Topical Bible for Kids

KJV

by

Michelle Brock

Illustrations by Anna Rose Pryde

Cover design by Bretta Watterson

Printed in the United States of America

Second Printing, 2016

ISBN 978-0-9969477-0-1

All Scripture quotations are from the authorized King James Version.

The text is set in Avenir, chosen specifically to be easily read by children.

www.as4me.net

Kids!

This book is for you.

There are a lot of great Bible verses that will help you and encourage you. If you don't find a topic you are looking for, then make your own list! There is room in the back of the book for your own Bible topic lists.

P.S. There are some notes for parents in the back of the book, too!

Table of Contents

Afraid

Related topics: Worry, Trust, Confidence

What time I am afraid, I will trust in thee. In God I will praise his word, in God I have put my trust; I will not fear what flesh can do unto me. Psalm 56:3-4

Praying helps me when I am afraid.

And call upon me in the day of trouble: I will deliver thee, and thou shalt glorify me. Psalm 50:15

Because God is all powerful, I can ask him to help me when I am afraid.

God is our refuge and strength, a very present help in trouble. Psalm 46:1

Fear thou not; for I am with thee: be not dismayed; for I am thy God: I will strengthen thee; yea, I will help thee; yea, I will uphold thee with the right hand of my righteousness. Isaiah 41:10

From the end of the earth will I cry unto thee, when my heart is overwhelmed: lead me to the rock that is higher than I. For thou hast been a shelter for me, and a strong tower from the enemy. Psalm 61:2-3

Because God takes care of me, I can sleep and not be afraid in the dark.

I will both lay me down in peace, and sleep: for thou, Lord, only makest me dwell in safety. Psalm 4:8

I learn to trust God when I remember that he is a Good Shepherd who loves me.

I am the good shepherd, and know my sheep. John 10:14a

The Lord is my shepherd; I shall not want. He maketh me to lie down in green pastures: he leadeth me beside the still waters. He restoreth my soul: he leadeth me in the paths of righteousness for his name's sake. Yea, though I walk through the valley of the shadow of death, I will fear no evil: for thou art with me; thy rod and thy staff they comfort me.
Psalm 23:1-4

Wisdom helps me to stop being fearful at bedtime.

My son, let not them depart from thine eyes: keep sound wisdom and discretion: So shall they be life unto thy soul, and grace to thy neck. Then shalt thou walk in thy way safely, and thy foot shall not stumble. When thou liest down, thou shalt not be afraid: yea, thou shalt lie down, and thy sleep shall be sweet. Proverbs 3:21-24

Because storms obey God, I can trust him during thunderstorms!

And there arose a great storm of wind, and the waves beat into the ship, so that it was now full. And he [Jesus] was in the hinder part of the ship, asleep on a pillow: and they awake him, and say unto him, Master, carest thou not that we perish? And he arose, and rebuked the wind, and said unto the sea, Peace, be still. And the wind ceased, and there was a great calm. Mark 4:37-39

I can pray for boldness (even when I am afraid) like the first Christians.

And now, Lord, behold their threatenings: and grant unto thy servants, that with all boldness they may speak thy word, By stretching forth thine hand to heal; and that signs and wonders may be done by the name of thy holy child Jesus. And when they had prayed, the place was shaken where they were assembled together; and they were all filled with the Holy Ghost, and they spake the word of God with boldness. Acts 4:29-31

Because God made me, he knows all about my weaknesses and can help me.

And Moses said unto the Lord, O my Lord, I am not eloquent, neither heretofore, nor since thou hast spoken unto thy servant: but I am slow of speech, and of a slow tongue. And the Lord said unto him, Who hath made man's mouth? or who maketh the dumb, or deaf, or the seeing, or the blind? have not I the Lord? Now therefore go, and I will be with thy mouth, and teach thee what thou shalt say. Exodus 4:10-12

Faithful is he that calleth you, who also will do it. 1 Thessalonians 5:24

The Lord will perfect that which concerneth me: thy mercy, O Lord, endureth for ever: forsake not the works of thine own hands. Psalm 138:8

Elijah's servant was afraid until he realized that God was more powerful than his enemies. 2 Kings 6:15-23 (See Psalm 34:7)

Asa was a king who was afraid of a big army, and he prayed for help. God delivered him because he relied on God's help. 2 Chronicles 14:11-12

ANGER

Related topics: Patience, Forgiveness, Humility, Selfish

Anger can come from selfish desires.

For the wrath of man worketh not the righteousness of God. James 1:20

He that is slow to anger is better than the mighty; and he that ruleth his spirit than he that taketh a city. Proverbs 16:32

It is better to dwell in the wilderness, than with a contentious and an angry woman. Proverbs 21:19

Make no friendship with an angry man; and with a furious man thou shalt not go: Lest thou learn his ways, and get a snare to thy soul. Proverbs 22:24-25

Because God forgave me, I am learning to be kind and forgiving instead of angry.

A soft answer turneth away wrath: but grievous words stir up anger. The tongue of the wise useth knowledge aright: but the mouth of fools poureth out foolishness. Proverbs 15:1-2

Let all bitterness, and wrath, and anger, and clamour, and evil speaking, be put away from you, with all malice: And be ye kind one to another, tenderhearted, forgiving one another, even as God for Christ's sake hath forgiven you. Ephesians 4:31-32

I can be slow to anger by learning to ask questions instead of talking, and then listening to the answers.

Wherefore, my beloved brethren, let every man be swift to hear, slow to speak, slow to wrath. James 1:19

Impatience that comes from pride often leads to anger.

Better is the end of a thing than the beginning thereof: and the patient in spirit is better than the proud in spirit. Be not hasty in thy spirit to be angry: for anger resteth in the bosom of fools. Ecclesiastes 7:8-9

I learn patience by learning to trust God.

Rest in the Lord, and wait patiently for him: fret not thyself because of him who prospereth in his way, because of the man who bringeth wicked devices to pass. Psalm 37:7

Cease from anger, and forsake wrath: fret not thyself in any wise to do evil. For evildoers shall be cut off: but those that wait upon the Lord, they shall inherit the earth. Psalm 37:8-9

> Balaam was angry with his donkey. He didn't know God used his donkey to protect him. Numbers 22:21-35 (Sometimes I am angry when I don't get my own way, and I forget that God uses my circumstances for good.)
>
> Jonah was angry because God forgave people he hated. Jonah 4:1-4

BAPTISM

Jesus wants his disciples to be baptized.

And Jesus came and spake unto them, saying, All power is given unto me in heaven and in earth. Go ye therefore, and teach all nations, baptizing them in the name of the Father, and of the Son, and of the Holy Ghost: Teaching them to observe all things whatsoever I have commanded you: and, lo, I am with you always, even unto the end of the world. Amen. Matthew 28:18-20

Christians are baptized after they are saved.

But when they believed Philip preaching the things concerning the kingdom of God, and the name of Jesus Christ, they were baptized, both men and women. Acts 8:12

And as they went on their way, they came unto a certain water: and the eunuch said, See, here is water; what doth hinder me to be baptized? And he commanded the chariot to stand still: and they went down both into the water, both Philip and the eunuch; and he baptized him. And when they were come up out of the water, the Spirit of the Lord caught away Philip, that the eunuch saw him no more: and he went on his way rejoicing. Acts 8:36, 38-39

Baptism is how the first Christians began to be a part of a local church.

Then they that gladly received his word were baptized: and the same day there were added unto them about three thousand souls. And they continued stedfastly in the apostles' doctrine and fellowship, and in breaking of bread, and in prayers. Acts 2:41-42

Baptism is a way of telling the story of the gospel, and telling others that Jesus has saved us, and that we want to follow him.

Know ye not, that so many of us as were baptized into Jesus Christ were baptized into his death? Therefore we are buried with him by baptism into death: that like as Christ was raised up from the dead by the glory of the Father, even so we also should walk in newness of life. For if we have been planted together in the likeness of his death, we shall be also in the likeness of his resurrection. Romans 6:3-5

BEAUTY

The Bible tells me that God is beautiful! Everything else that is beautiful is like him!

One thing have I desired of the Lord, that will I seek after; that I may dwell in the house of the Lord all the days of my life, to behold the beauty of the Lord, and to enquire in his temple. Psalm 27:4

God will make everything beautiful when he is ready, including me!

He hath made every thing beautiful in his time. Ecclesiastes 3:11

Outside beauty is not nearly as important as the beauty of loving and fearing God!

Favour is deceitful, and beauty is vain: but a woman that feareth the Lord, she shall be praised. Give her of the fruit of her hands; and let her own works praise her in the gates. Proverbs 31:30-31

But the Lord said unto Samuel, Look not on his countenance, or on the height of his stature; because I have refused him: for the Lord seeth not as man seeth; for man looketh on the outward appearance, but the Lord looketh on the heart. 1 Samuel 16:7

God loves the beauty of a gentle and quiet spirit!

But let [your beauty] be the hidden man of the heart, in that which is not corruptible, even the ornament of a meek and quiet spirit, which is in the sight of God of great price. 1 Peter 3:4

God makes attractive people. It's all mixed up if those people aren't attractive inside, too.

As a jewel of gold in a swine's snout, so is a fair woman which is without discretion. Proverbs 11:22

Holiness is beautiful!

Give unto the Lord the glory due unto his name; worship the Lord in the beauty of holiness. Psalm 29:2

Salvation is beautiful!

I will greatly rejoice in the Lord, my soul shall be joyful in my God; for he hath clothed me with the garments of salvation, he hath covered me with the robe of righteousness, as a bridegroom decketh himself with ornaments, and as a bride adorneth herself with her jewels. Isaiah 61:10

How beautiful are the feet of them that preach the gospel of peace, and bring glad tidings of good things!
Romans 10:15b

Can a maid forget her ornaments, or a bride her attire? yet my people have forgotten me days without number.
Jeremiah 2:32

Bible Study

The Bible shows me my motives and what God wants me to change.

For the word of God is quick, and powerful, and sharper than any twoedged sword, piercing even to the dividing asunder of soul and spirit, and of the joints and marrow, and is a discerner of the thoughts and intents of the heart. Hebrews 4:12

Even a child who cannot read well can obey what he knows is true.

For Ezra had prepared his heart to seek the law of the Lord, and to do it, and to teach in Israel statues and judgments. Ezra 7:10

I like to think about the Bible.

Thy words were found, and I did eat them; and thy word was unto me the joy and rejoicing of mine heart: for I am called by thy name, O Lord God of hosts. Jeremiah 15:16

Thy testimonies also are my delight and my counselors. Psalm 119:24

I will meditate in thy precepts, and have respect unto thy ways. I will delight myself in thy statutes: I will not forget thy word. Psalm 119:15-16

I want to learn to understand and love the Bible.

But his delight is in the law of the Lord; and in his law doth he meditate day and night. And he shall be like a tree planted by the rivers of water, that bringeth forth his fruit in his season; his leaf also shall not wither; and whatsoever he doeth shall prosper. Psalm 1:2-3

Praise ye the Lord. Blessed is the man that feareth the Lord, that delighteth greatly in his commandments.
Psalm 112:1

Knowing this first, that no prophecy of the scripture is of any private interpretation. For the prophecy came not in old time by the will of man: but holy men of God spake as they were moved by the Holy Ghost. 2 Peter 1:20-21

The Holy Spirit uses the Bible to teach God's children.

And take the helmet of salvation, and the sword of the Spirit, which is the word of God. Ephesians 6:17

Some things in the Bible are hard to understand, even for adults!

And account that the longsuffering of our Lord is salvation; even as our beloved brother Paul also according to the wisdom given unto him hath written unto you; As also in all his epistles, speaking in them of these things; in which are some things hard to be understood, which they that are unlearned and unstable wrest, as they do also the other scriptures, unto their own destruction. 2 Peter 3:15-16

Psalm 119 is the longest chapter in the Bible, and it is all about the Bible. See if you can find all the different words King David used to refer to the Bible.

Birds

God uses birds to teach me what he is like!

But they that wait upon the Lord shall renew their strength; they shall mount up with wings as eagles; they shall run, and not be weary; and they shall walk, and not faint. Isaiah 40:31

Are not two sparrows sold for a farthing? and one of them shall not fall on the ground without your Father. But the very hairs of your head are all numbered. Fear ye not therefore, ye are of more value than many sparrows. Matthew 10:29-31

Doth the hawk fly by thy wisdom, and stretch her wings toward the south? Doth the eagle mount up at thy command, and make her nest on high? She dwelleth and abideth on the rock, upon the crag of the rock, and the strong place. From thence she seeketh the prey, and her eyes behold afar off. Her young ones also suck up blood: and where the slain are, there is she. Job 39:26-30

Behold the fowls of the air: for they sow not, neither do they reap, nor gather into barns; yet your heavenly Father feedeth them. Are ye not much better than they? But seek ye first the kingdom of God, and his righteousness; and all these things shall be added unto you. Matthew 6:26, 33

He that dwelleth in the secret place of the most High shall abide under the shadow of the Almighty. I will say of the Lord, He is my refuge and my fortress: my God; in him will I trust. Surely he shall deliver thee from the snare of the fowler, and from the noisome pestilence. He shall cover thee with his feathers, and under his wings shalt thou trust: his truth shall be thy shield and buckler. Psalm 91:1-4

Bless the Lord, O my soul, and forget not all his benefits: Who forgiveth all thine iniquities; who healeth all thy diseases; Who redeemeth thy life from destruction; who crowneth thee with lovingkindness and tender mercies; Who satisfieth thy mouth with good things; so that thy youth is renewed like the eagle's. Psalm 103:2-5

Sing unto the Lord with thanksgiving; sing praise upon the harp unto our God: Who covereth the heaven with clouds, who prepareth rain for the earth, who maketh grass to grow upon the mountains. He giveth to the beast his food, and to the young ravens which cry. Psalm 147:7-9

Bullies

Related topic: Mean People

God sees when I am mistreated.

But whoso shall offend one of these little ones which believe in me, it were better for him that a millstone were hanged about his neck, and that he were drowned in the depth of the sea. Matthew 18:5-6

God will help me not be silent when I see someone being bullied.

Open thy mouth, judge righteously, and plead the cause of the poor and needy. Proverbs 31:9

Learn to do well; seek judgment, relieve the oppressed, judge the fatherless, plead for the widow. Isaiah 1:17

Take counsel, execute judgment; make thy shadow as the night in the midst of the noonday; hide the outcasts; bewray [betray] not him that wandereth. Let mine outcasts dwell with thee, be thou a cover to them from the face of the spoiler. Isaiah 16:3-4

I can follow Jesus' example to help those who are weaker than I am.

We then that are strong ought to bear the infirmities of the weak, and not to please ourselves. Let every one of us please his neighbour for his good to edification. For even Christ pleased not himself; but, as it is written, The reproaches of them that reproached thee fell on me. Romans 15:1-3

For thou hast been a strength to the poor, a strength to the needy in his distress, a refuge from the storm, a shadow from the heat, when the blast of the terrible ones is as a storm against the wall. Isaiah 25:4

Unto the upright there ariseth light in the darkness; he is gracious, and full of compassion, and righteous. Psalm 112:4

God wants me to tell someone in authority when someone is trying to hurt me or someone else.

And when Paul's sister's son heard of their lying in wait [planning to kill him], he went and entered into the castle, and told Paul. Then Paul called one of the centurions unto him, and said, Bring this young man unto the chief captain: for he hath a certain thing to tell him. Acts 23:16-17

God wants me to pray for bullies.

Ye have heard that it hath been said, Thou shalt love thy neighbour, and hate thine enemy. But I say unto you, Love your enemies, bless them that curse you, do good to them that hate you, and pray for them which despitefully use you, and persecute you; That ye may be the children of your Father which is in heaven: for he maketh his sun to rise on the evil and on the good, and sendeth rain on the just and on the unjust. Matthew 5:43-45

God does not want me to "get back at" bullies, or take revenge when I am wronged.

Dearly beloved, avenge not yourselves, but rather give place unto wrath: for it is written, Vengeance is mine; I will repay, saith the Lord. Therefore if thine enemy hunger, feed him; if he thirst, give him drink: for in so doing thou shalt heap coals of fire on his head. Be not overcome of evil, but overcome evil with good. Romans 12:19-21

King David wrote Psalm 35 when he was dealing with enemies.

CHILDREN

Even a child is known by his doings, whether his work be pure, and whether it be right. Proverbs 20:11

Jesus loves to hear me talk to him.

Then were there brought unto him little children, that he should put his hands on them, and pray: and the disciples rebuked them. But Jesus said, Suffer little children, and forbid them not, to come unto me: for of such is the kingdom of heaven. And he laid his hands on them, and departed thence. Matthew 19:13-15

God can use me by my example to others.

Let no man despise thy youth; but be thou an example of the believers, in word, in conversation, in charity, in spirit, in faith, in purity. 1 Timothy 4:12

God's Word is for children, too!

Gather the people together, men and women, and children, and thy stranger that is within thy gates, that they may hear, and that they may learn, and fear the Lord your God, and observe to do all the words of this law: Deuteronomy 31:12

The secret things belong unto the Lord our God, but those things which are revealed belong unto us and to our children for ever, that we may do all the words of this law. Deuteronomy 29:29

Timothy learned the Bible as a child, and stayed faithful as an adult! 2 Timothy 3:14-17

Jesus reminded the people that God's truth is spoken by children! Matthew 21:15-16

Chores

Related topic: Work

God wants me to be a good steward, and learn to take care of my things.

Let all things be done decently and in order.
1 Corinthians 14:40

Be thou diligent to know the state of thy flocks, and look well to thy herds. Proverbs 27:23

The slothful man roasteth not that which he took in hunting: but the substance of a diligent man is precious.
Proverbs 12:27

Moreover it is required in stewards, that a man be found faithful. 1 Corinthians 4:2

And he said unto him, Well, thou good servant: because thou hast been faithful in a very little, have thou authority over ten cities. Luke 19:17

Whether therefore ye eat, or drink, or whatsoever ye do, do all to the glory of God. 1 Corinthians 10:31

I am encouraged when I remember that God will reward my hard work.

And let us not be weary in well doing: for in due season we shall reap, if we faint not. Galatians 6:9

And whatsoever ye do, do it heartily, as to the Lord, and not unto men; Colossians 3:23

God wants me to work so that I can do good for others.

I have shewed you all things, how that so labouring ye ought to support the weak, and to remember the words of the Lord Jesus, how he said, It is more blessed to give than to receive.
Acts 20:35

Complaining

Related topics: Thankfulness, Contentment

Do all things without murmurings [complaining] and disputings. Philippians 2:14

Neither murmur ye, as some of them also murmured, and were destroyed of the destroyer. 1 Corinthians 10:10

I complain when I forget that God is good.

They kept not the covenant of God, and refused to walk in his law; And forgat his works, and his wonders that he had shewed them. Marvellous things did he in the sight of their fathers, in the land of Egypt, in the field of Zoan. He divided the sea, and caused them to pass through; and he made the waters to stand as an heap. In the daytime also he led them with a cloud, and all the night with a light of fire. He clave the rocks in the wilderness, and gave them drink as out of the great depths. He brought streams also out of the rock, and caused waters to run down like rivers. And they sinned yet more against him by provoking the most High in the wilderness. And they tempted God in their heart by asking meat for their lust. Psalm 78:10-18

I am helped when I remember what God has done for me and given me, instead of complaining!

The Lord heareth your murmurings which ye murmur against him: and what are we? your murmurings are not against us, but against the Lord. Exodus 16:8b

Give thanks unto the Lord, call upon his name, make known his deeds among the people. Sing unto him, sing psalms unto him, talk ye of all his wondrous works. Glory ye in his holy name: let the heart of them rejoice that seek the Lord. Seek the Lord and his strength, seek his face continually. Remember his marvellous works that he hath done, his wonders, and the judgments of his mouth; 1 Chronicles 16:8-12

Communion (The Lord's Supper)

Christians take communion to tell others that Jesus has saved them.

For as often as ye eat this bread, and drink this cup, ye do shew the Lord's death till he come. 1 Corinthians 11:26

Christians take communion to remember Jesus' death on the cross.

For I have received of the Lord that which also I delivered unto you, that the Lord Jesus the same night in which he was betrayed took bread: And when he had given thanks, he brake it, and said, Take, eat: this is my body, which is broken for you: this do in remembrance of me. After the same manner also he took the cup, when he had supped, saying, this cup is the new testament in my blood: this do ye, as oft as ye drink it, in remembrance of me. 1 Corinthians 11:23-25

Christians take communion with respect.

Wherefore whosoever shall eat this bread, and drink this cup of the Lord, unworthily, shall be guilty of the body and blood of the Lord. But let a man examine himself, and so let him eat of that bread, and drink of that cup. 1 Corinthians 11:27-28

CONFIDENCE

Related topics: Afraid, Shy, Self-Esteem, Faith

Because God loves me and takes care of me, I can be confident!

Have not I commanded thee? Be strong and of a good courage; be not afraid, neither be thou dismayed: for the Lord thy God is with thee whithersoever thou goest. Joshua 1:9

In the fear of the Lord is strong confidence: and his children shall have a place of refuge. Proverbs 14:26

The wicked flee when no man pursueth: but the righteous are bold as a lion. Proverbs 28:1

Who is as the wise man? and who knoweth the interpretation of a thing? a man's wisdom maketh his face to shine, and the boldness of his face shall be changed. Ecclesiastes 8:1

I had fainted, unless I had believed to see the goodness of the Lord in the land of the living. Wait on the Lord: be of good courage, and he shall strengthen thine heart: wait, I say, on the Lord. Psalm 27:13-14

Fear thou not; for I am with thee: be not dismayed; for I am thy God: I will strengthen thee; yea, I will help thee; yea, I will uphold thee with the right hand of my righteousness. Isaiah 41:10

Because Jesus understands my weaknesses, I can be confident that he will help me when I come to him.

Let us therefore come boldly unto the throne of grace, that we may obtain mercy, and find grace to help in time of need. Hebrews 4:16.

I can help others trust God and be confident, too!

They helped every one his neighbour; and every one said to his brother, Be of good courage. Isaiah 41:6

I will have confidence when I am walking with God.

And now, little children, abide in him; that, when he shall appear, we may have confidence, and not be ashamed before him at his coming. 1 John 2:28

> Peter's confidence in Jesus helped him not to be afraid, and to walk on top of water. Matthew 14:25-33

Contentment

Related topics: Thankfulness, Fairness, Envy/ Jealousy

Because God is good, I can be content even when I don't get what I want.

All the days of the afflicted are evil: but he that is of a merry heart hath a continual feast. Better is little with the fear of the Lord than great treasure and trouble therewith. Better is a dinner of herbs where love is, than a stalled ox and hatred therewith. Proverbs 15:15-17

For the Lord God is a sun and shield: the Lord will give grace and glory: no good thing will he withhold from them that walk uprightly. O Lord of hosts, blessed is the man that trusteth in thee. Psalm 84:11-12

Because God is always with me, I can be content even when I don't get what I what.

Let your conversation be without covetousness; and be content with such things as ye have: for he hath said, I will never leave thee, nor forsake thee. Hebrews 13:5

Contentment is difficult to learn, even for adults.

Not that I speak in respect of want: for I have learned, in whatsoever state I am, therewith to be content. Philippians 4:11

And having food and raiment let us be therewith content. 1 Timothy 6:8

CREATION

In the beginning God created the heaven and the earth. Genesis 1:1

Through faith we understand that the worlds were framed by the word of God, so that things which are seen were not made of things which do appear. Hebrews 11:3

Because God created everything, I know he can do anything.

Ah Lord God! behold, thou hast made the heaven and the earth by thy great power and stretched out arm, and there is nothing too hard for thee: Jeremiah 32:17

Jesus told us that God made Adam and Eve.

And he answered and said unto them, Have ye not read, that he which made them at the beginning made them male and female? Matthew 19:4

God owns everything that he has created, even me!

Know ye that the Lord he is God: it is he that hath made us, and not we ourselves; we are his people, and the sheep of his pasture. Psalm 100:3

The earth is the Lord's, and the fulness thereof; the world, and they that dwell therein. For he hath founded it upon the seas, and established it upon the floods. Psalm 24:1-2

Sin ruins God's creation.

And God saw that the wickedness of man was great in the earth, and that every imagination of the thoughts of his heart was only evil continually. And it repented the Lord that he had made man on the earth, and it grieved him at his heart. Genesis 6:5-6

Jesus came to repair his creation.

For by grace are ye saved through faith; and that not of yourselves: it is the gift of God: Not of works, lest any man should boast. For we are his workmanship, created in Christ Jesus unto good works, which God hath before ordained that we should walk in them. Ephesians 2:8-10

Therefore if any man be in Christ, he is a new creature: old things are passed away; behold, all things are become new. 2 Corinthians 5:17

The Lord will perfect that which concerneth me: thy mercy, O Lord, endureth for ever: forsake not the works of thine own hands. Psalm 138:8

God created all things for his own glory and pleasure.

Thou art worthy, O Lord, to receive glory and honour and power: for thou hast created all things, and for thy pleasure they are and were created. Revelation 4:11

For by him were all things created, that are in heaven, and that are in earth, visible and invisible, whether they be thrones, or dominions, or principalities, or powers: all things were created by him, and for him: Colossians 1:16

Death

Related topics: Heaven

When someone I love dies and I am hurting, God promises to stay with me because he is a good shepherd.

Yea, though I walk through the valley of the shadow of death, I will fear no evil: for thou art with me; thy rod and thy staff they comfort me. Psalm 23:4

God understands and shares my grief.

The Lord is nigh unto them that are of a broken heart; and saveth such as be of a contrite spirit. Psalm 34:18

Then when Mary was come where Jesus was, and saw him, she fell down at his feet, saying unto him, Lord, if thou hadst been here, my brother had not died. When Jesus therefore saw her weeping, and the Jews also weeping which came with her, he groaned in the spirit, and was troubled. And said, Where have ye laid him? They said unto him, Lord, come and see. Jesus wept. Then said the Jews, Behold how he loved him! John 11:32-36

Blessed be God, even the Father of our Lord Jesus Christ, the Father of mercies, and the God of all comfort; Who comforteth us in all our tribulation, that we may be able to comfort them which are in any trouble, by the comfort wherewith we ourselves are comforted of God.
2 Corinthians 1:3-4

After a Christian dies, he is with Jesus in heaven.

For I am in a strait betwixt two, having a desire to depart, and to be with Christ; which is far better: Nevertheless to abide in the flesh is more needful for you. Philippians 1:23-24

We are confident, I say, and willing rather to be absent from the body, and to be present with the Lord. Wherefore we labour, that, whether present or absent, we may be accepted of him. 2 Corinthians 5:8-9

The reason we have death is because of sin.

Wherefore, as by one man sin entered into the world, and death by sin; and so death passed upon all men, for that all have sinned: Romans 5:12

But every man is tempted, when he is drawn away of his own lust, and enticed. Then when lust hath conceived, it bringeth forth sin: and sin, when it is finished, bringeth forth death.
James 1:14-15

Death of a Pet

Related topics: Death, Pets

God cares about what happens to even the smallest animals.

Are not five sparrows sold for two farthings, and not one of them is forgotten before God? Luke 12:6

Six days thou shalt do thy work, and on the seventh day thou shalt rest: [so] that thine ox and thine ass may rest, and the son of thy handmaid, and the stranger, may be refreshed. Exodus 23:12

But ask now the beasts, and they shall teach thee; and the fowls of the air, and they shall tell thee: Or speak to the earth, and it shall teach thee: and the fishes of the sea shall declare unto thee. Who knoweth not in all these that the hand of the Lord hath wrought this? In [God's] hand is the soul of every living thing, and the breath of all mankind. Job 12:7-10

For every beast of the forest is mine, and the cattle upon a thousand hills. I know all the fowls of the mountains: and the wild beasts of the field are mine. Psalm 50:10-11

Because God takes care of the birds, I know he will take care of me, too.

Behold the fowls of the air: for they sow not, neither do they reap, nor gather into barns; yet your heavenly Father feedeth them. Are ye not much better than they? Matthew 6:26

God cares when I am sad.

Yea, though I walk through the valley of the shadow of death, I will fear no evil: for thou art with me; thy rod and thy staff they comfort me. Psalm 23:4

Although we love our pets very much when they are alive, we do not know what happens to them after they die.

Who knoweth the spirit of man that goeth upward, and the spirit of the beast that goeth downward to the earth? Ecclesiastes 3:21

DISABILITY

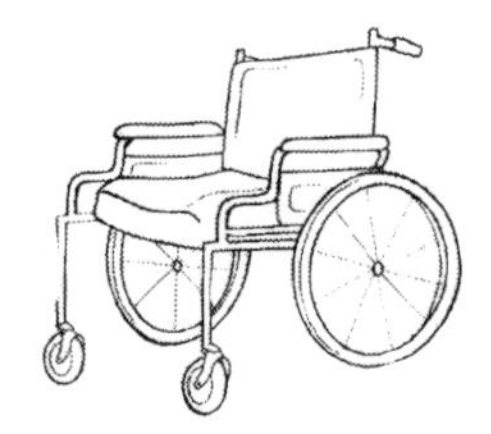

Related topics: Suffering, Self Esteem

God made each person with the abilities they need to serve him!

Moses said unto the Lord, O my Lord, I am not eloquent, neither heretofore, nor since thou hast spoken unto thy servant: but I am slow of speech, and of a slow tongue. And the Lord said unto him, Who hath made man's mouth? or who maketh the dumb, or deaf, or the seeing, or the blind? have not I the Lord? Now therefore go, and I will be with thy mouth, and teach thee what thou shalt say. Exodus 4:10-12

I will praise thee; for I am fearfully and wonderfully made: marvellous are thy works; and that my soul knoweth right well. Psalm 139:14

God will fix all the weaknesses and disabilities in heaven!

And God shall wipe away all tears from their eyes; and there shall be no more death, neither sorrow, nor crying, neither shall there be any more pain: for the former things are passed away. And he that sat upon the throne said, Behold, I make all things new. And he said unto me, Write: for these words are true and faithful. Revelation 21:4-5

Then the eyes of the blind shall be opened, and the ears of the deaf shall be unstopped. Then shall the lame man leap as an hart [stag], and the tongue of the dumb sing: for in the wilderness shall waters break out, and streams in the desert. Isaiah 35:5-6

God shows his power through our weaknesses and disabilities.

And as Jesus passed by, he saw a man which was blind from his birth. And his disciples asked him, saying, Master, who did sin, this man, or his parents, that he was born blind? Jesus answered, Neither hath this man sinned, nor his parents: but that the works of God should be made manifest in him. John 9:1-3

For this thing [Paul's problem] I besought the Lord thrice, that it might depart from me. And he said unto me, My grace is sufficient for thee: for my strength is made perfect in weakness. Most gladly therefore will I rather glory in my infirmities, that the power of Christ may rest upon me. Therefore I take pleasure in infirmities, in reproaches, in necessities, in persecutions, in distresses for Christ's sake: for when I am weak, then am I strong. 2 Corinthians 12:8-10

God gives different abilities to each person, and wants each person to use those abilities for him.

His Lord said unto him, Well done, good and faithful servant; thou hast been faithful over a few things, I will make thee ruler over many things: enter thou into the joy of thy Lord. Matthew 25:23

Read the whole story at Matthew 25:14-29.

Knowing and loving God is more important than being smart or strong.

He delighteth not in the strength of the horse: he taketh not pleasure in the legs of a man. The Lord taketh pleasure in them that fear him, in those that hope in his mercy. Psalm 147:10-11

DISAPPOINTMENT

Related topics: Contentment, God, Omnipotent

God is good, and he does not withhold good things from me.

For the Lord God is a sun and shield: the Lord will give grace and glory: no good thing will he withhold from them that walk uprightly. Psalm 84:11

Because God knows the future, I can trust him when I am disappointed.

And we know that all things work together for good to them that love God, to them who are the called according to his purpose. Romans 8:28

And Joseph said unto them [his brothers], Fear not: for am I in the place of God? But as for you, ye thought evil against me; but God meant it unto good, to bring to pass, as it is this day, to save much people alive. Genesis 50:19-20

And it came to pass, when Pharaoh had let the people go, that God led them not through the way of the land of the Philistines, although that was near; for God said, Lest peradventure [perhaps] the people repent when they see war, and they return to Egypt: But God led the people about, through the way of the wilderness of the Red sea: and the children of Israel went up harnessed out of the land of Egypt. Exodus 13:17-18

Because God is faithful, I can handle disappointment.

There hath no temptation taken you but such as is common to man: but God is faithful, who will not suffer you to be tempted above that ye are able; but will with the temptation also make a way to escape, that ye may be able to bear it. 1 Corinthians 10:13

Be careful for nothing; but in every thing by prayer and supplication with thanksgiving let your requests be made known unto God. And the peace of God, which passeth all understanding, shall keep your hearts and minds through Christ Jesus. Philippians 4:6-7

Trust in the Lord with all thine heart; and lean not unto thine own understanding. In all thy ways acknowledge him, and he shall direct thy paths. Proverbs 3:5-6

As for God, his way is perfect: the word of the Lord is tried: he is a buckler to all those that trust in him. Psalm 18:30

O taste and see that the Lord is good: blessed is the man that trusteth in him. Psalm 34:8

Although the fig tree shall not blossom, neither shall fruit be in the vines; the labour of the olive shall fail, and the fields shall yield no meat; the flock shall be cut off from the fold, and there shall be no herd in the stalls: Yet I will rejoice in the Lord, I will joy in the God of my salvation. Habakkuk 3:17-18

Examples of people who had disappointment: Hagar, Hannah, Esther, Ruth, Paul.

Psalm 34 and Psalm 46 are good Psalms to read when disappointed.

Divorce

See: Parents, Hope, Sadness, Suffering

Enemies

See Bullies, Mean People, Fighting, Forgiveness

Envy/ Jealousy

Related topics: Contentment, Fairness, Thankfulness

Envy is selfish and destructive.

A sound heart is the life of the flesh: but envy the rottenness of the bones. Proverbs 14:30

Let us not be desirous of vain glory, provoking one another, envying one another. Galatians 5:26

For where envying and strife is, there is confusion and every evil work. James 3:16

God does not want me to be envious of bad people, because their life has a sad ending.

Truly God is good to Israel, even to such as are of a clean heart. But as for me, my feet were almost gone; my steps had well nigh slipped. For I was envious at the foolish, when I saw the prosperity of the wicked. Until I went into the sanctuary of God; then understood I their end.
Psalm 73:1-3, 17

God wants me to learn to trust him with the things or friends I want to have.

Rest in the Lord, and wait patiently for him: fret not thyself because of him who prospereth in his way, because of the man who bringeth wicked devices to pass. Psalm 37:7

Be not thou envious against evil men, neither desire to be with them. For their heart studieth destruction, and their lips talk of mischief. Proverbs 24:1-2

Envy destroys family relationships.

And the patriarchs, moved with envy, sold Joseph into Egypt: but God was with him. Acts 7:9 (See also Genesis 37.)

And when Rachel saw that she bare Jacob no children, Rachel envied her sister; and said unto Jacob, Give me children, or else I die. And Jacob's anger was kindled against Rachel: and he said, Am I in God's stead, who hath withheld from thee the fruit of the womb? Genesis 30:1-2

Envy hurts God's helpers.

And there ran a young man, and told Moses, and said, Eldad and Medad do prophesy in the camp. And Joshua the son of Nun, the servant of Moses, one of his young men, answered and said, My Lord Moses, forbid them. And Moses said unto him, Enviest thou for my sake? would God that all the Lord's people were prophets, and that the Lord would put his spirit upon them! Numbers 11:27-29

Envy causes people to do bad things. For examples, see Mark 15:9-10 and Acts 17:5.

Miriam and Aaron were envious of Moses. Numbers 12:1-15

Evangelism (Telling People about Jesus)

I show others that I follow Jesus when I love other Christians.

By this shall all men know that ye are my disciples, if ye have love one to another. John 13:35

I please God when I tell what he has done and is doing in my life.

O give thanks unto the Lord; call upon his name: make known his deeds among the people. Sing unto him, sing psalms unto him: talk ye of all his wondrous works. Glory ye in his holy name: let the heart of them rejoice that seek the Lord. Seek the Lord, and his strength: seek his face evermore. Remember his marvellous works that he hath done; his wonders, and the judgments of his mouth; Psalm 105:1-5

Go ye therefore, and teach all nations, baptizing them in the name of the Father, and of the Son, and of the Holy Ghost: Teaching them to observe all things whatsoever I have commanded you: and, lo, I am with you always, even unto the end of the world. Amen. Matthew 28:19-20

I tell other people about God by living like Jesus.

Even a child is known by his doings, whether his work be pure, and whether it be right. Proverbs 20:11

Let your light so shine before men, that they may see your good works, and glorify your Father which is in heaven. Matthew 5:16

Do all things without murmurings and disputings: That ye may be blameless and harmless, the sons of God, without rebuke, in the midst of a crooked and perverse nation, among whom ye shine as lights in the world; Holding forth the word of life; that I may rejoice in the day of Christ, that I have not run in vain, neither laboured in vain. Philippians 2:14-16

But I say unto you, Love your enemies, bless them that curse you, do good to them that hate you, and pray for them which despitefully use you, and persecute you; That ye may be the children of your Father which is in heaven: for he maketh his sun to rise on the evil and on the good, and sendeth rain on the just and on the unjust. For if ye love them which love you, what reward have ye? do not even the publicans the same? And if ye salute your brethren only, what do ye more than others? do not even the publicans so?
Matthew 5:44-47

Psalm 96 tells God's people to tell others about their wonderful God.

See how God uses children in his plans.
Naaman (2 Kings 5:2-15), Rhoda (Acts 12:13-17)
The little boy who shared his lunch (John 6:9-14).

Fairness

Related topics: Anger, Envy, Humility, Contentment

God is just. He gives each person what is right, even though it may be different.

Now there are diversities of gifts, but the same Spirit.
1 Corinthians 12:4

For God is not unrighteous to forget your work and labour of love, which ye have shewed toward his name, in that ye have ministered to the saints, and do minister. Hebrews 6:10

O let the nations be glad and sing for joy: for thou shalt judge the people righteously, and govern the nations upon earth. Selah. Psalm 67:4

Jesus does not want me to fight about fairness. He wants me to remember that the best things are not things I can hold.

And one of the company said unto him [Jesus], Master, speak to my brother, that he divide the inheritance with me. And he said unto him, Man, who made me a judge or a divider over you? And he said unto them, Take heed, and beware of covetousness: for a man's life consisteth not in the abundance of the things which he possesseth. Luke 12:13-15

But they measuring themselves by themselves, and comparing themselves among themselves, are not wise.
2 Corinthians 10:12b

God wants me to look for ways that I can help and please others, before I look for ways to please myself. Jesus set the example for me to follow.

Look not every man on his own things, but every man also on the things of others. Philippians 2:4

We then that are strong ought to bear the infirmities of the weak, and not to please ourselves. Let every one of us please his neighbor for his good to edification. For even Christ pleased not himself. Romans 15:1-3a

And he came to Capernaum: and being in the house he asked them, What was it that ye disputed among yourselves by the way? But they held their peace: for by the way they had disputed among themselves, who should be the greatest. And he sat down, and called the twelve, and saith unto them, If any man desire to be first, the same shall be last of all, and servant of all. Mark 9:33-35

God does not want his children treating each other unfairly and dishonestly.

Have we not all one father? hath not one God created us? why do we deal treacherously every man against his brother, by profaning the covenant of our fathers? Malachi 2:10

A false balance [cheating] is abomination to the Lord: but a just weight [honesty] is his delight. Proverbs 11:1

He hath shewed thee, O man, what is good; and what doth the Lord require of thee, but to do justly, and to love mercy, and to walk humbly with thy God? Micah 6:8

> See Matthew 20:1-15 for a story about God's justice and differences.
>
> Paul helps the whole church in Corinth learn about fairness and differences in 1 Corinthians 12.
>
> Read about an older brother had problems being too worried about fairness. Luke 15:11-32

Faith

Related topic: Trust

Faith is believing what God says.

For what saith the scripture? Abraham believed God, and it was counted unto him for righteousness. Romans 4:3

God is faithful. I can have faith in him.

But without faith it is impossible to please him: for he that cometh to God must believe that he is, and that he is a rewarder of them that diligently seek him. Hebrews 11:6

For we walk by faith, not by sight. 2 Corinthians 5:7

Through faith also Sara herself received strength to conceive seed, and was delivered of a child when she was past age, because she judged him faithful who had promised. Hebrews 11:11

Therefore we conclude that a man is justified by faith without the deeds of the law. Romans 3:28

Faith comes from God.

Looking unto Jesus the author and finisher of our faith. Hebrews 12:2a

And the apostles said unto the Lord, Increase our faith. Luke 17:5

For by grace are ye saved through faith; and that not of yourselves: it is the gift of God: Not of works, lest any man should boast. Ephesians 2:8-9

Faith is remembering what God has done in the past, and believing he will work in the future.

I will remember the works of the Lord: surely I will remember thy wonders of old. I will meditate also of all thy work, and talk of thy doings. Psalm 77:11-12

Cause me to hear thy lovingkindness in the morning; for in thee do I trust: cause me to know the way wherein I should walk; for I lift up my soul unto thee. Psalm 143: 8

That the generation to come might know them, The children who would be born, That they may arise and declare them to their children, That they may set their hope in God, And not forget the works of God, But keep His commandments; And may not be like their fathers, A stubborn and rebellious generation, A generation that did not set its heart aright, And whose spirit was not faithful to God. Psalm 78:6-8

The Holy Spirit increases my faith when I listen to the Bible.

So then faith cometh by hearing, and hearing by the word of God. Romans 10:17

Faith helps me to obey even when I don't understand all the details.

By faith Abraham, when he was called to go out into a place which he should after receive for an inheritance, obeyed; and he went out, not knowing whither he went. Hebrews 11:8

Above all, taking the shield of faith, wherewith ye shall be able to quench all the fiery darts of the wicked. Ephesians 6:16

And seek not ye what ye shall eat, or what ye shall drink, neither be ye of doubtful mind. For all these things do the nations of the world seek after: and your Father knoweth that ye have need of these things. But rather seek ye the kingdom of God; and all these things shall be added unto you. Luke 12:29-31

Consider the ravens: for they neither sow nor reap; which neither have storehouse nor barn; and God feedeth them: how much more are ye better than the fowls? And which of you with taking thought can add to his stature one cubit? If ye then be not able to do that thing which is least, why take ye thought for the rest? Luke 12:24-26

Consider the lilies how they grow: they toil not, they spin not; and yet I say unto you, that Solomon in all his glory was not arrayed like one of these. If then God so clothe the grass, which is to day in the field, and to morrow is cast into the oven; how much more will he clothe you, O ye of little faith? Luke 12:27-28

Without faith, I am fearful.

And his disciples came to him, and awoke him, saying, Lord, save us: we perish. And he saith unto them, Why are ye fearful, O ye of little faith? Then he arose, and rebuked the winds and the sea; and there was a great calm. But the men marvelled, saying, What manner of man is this, that even the winds and the sea obey him! Matthew 8:24-27

> The Roman soldier had great faith because he knew Jesus had the authority to heal his servant, even from far away. Matthew 8:5-10
>
> A woman asked Jesus to help her daughter because she believed he was God, and that he was good. Matthew 15:22-28

FEAR

See Afraid

Fear of God

Related topic: Wisdom

In the fear of the Lord is strong confidence: and his children shall have a place of refuge. Proverbs 14:26

He giveth to the beast his food, and to the young ravens which cry. He delighteth not in the strength of the horse: he taketh not pleasure in the legs of a man. The Lord taketh pleasure in them that fear him, in those that hope in his mercy. Psalm 147:9-11

God wants me to learn about the fear of God

Come, ye children, hearken unto me: I will teach you the fear of the Lord. Psalm 34:11

Knowing and loving God's goodness and greatness helps me fear God!

For thou art great, and doest wondrous things: thou art God alone. Teach me thy way, O Lord; I will walk in thy truth: unite my heart to fear thy name. I will praise thee, O Lord my God, with all my heart: and I will glorify thy name for evermore. Psalm 86:11-12

If thou, Lord, shouldest mark iniquities, O Lord, who shall stand? But there is forgiveness with thee, that thou mayest be feared. Psalm 130:3-4

Knowing God's justice helps me fear God. He rewards my actions, both good and bad.

And all men shall fear, and shall declare the work of God; for they shall wisely consider of his doing. Psalm 64:9

Be not deceived; God is not mocked: for whatsoever a man soweth, that shall he also reap. Galatians 6:7

By the fear of the Lord men depart from evil. Proverbs 16:6b

God promises that I will learn how to fear God when I search for wisdom!

The fear of the Lord is the beginning of wisdom!
Proverbs 9:10a

So that thou incline thine ear unto wisdom, and apply thine heart to understanding; Yea, if thou criest after knowledge, and liftest up thy voice for understanding; If thou seekest her as silver, and searchest for her as for hid treasures; Then shalt thou understand the fear of the Lord, and find the knowledge of God. Proverbs 2:2-5

The fear of the Lord is to hate evil: pride, and arrogancy, and the evil way, and the froward mouth, do I hate. Proverbs 8:13

When I have the fear of God, I will not want to run away from Him.

And I will make an everlasting covenant with them, that I will not turn away from them, to do them good; but I will put my fear in their hearts, that they shall not depart from me.
Jeremiah 32:40

Ananias and Sapphira lied to God. When they died because of their sin, many people feared God. Acts 5:1-11

When God protected Daniel in the lion's den, Darius decreed that all people were to tremble and fear before the God of Daniel. Daniel 6, especially verses 26 and 27.

Fighting (strife)

Related topics: Forgiveness, Enemies, Mean People

Behold, how good and how pleasant it is for brethren to dwell together in unity! Psalm 133:1

Only by pride cometh contention: but with the well advised is wisdom. Proverbs 13:10

From whence come wars and fightings among you? come they not hence, even of your lusts that war in your members? James 4:1

Be kindly affectioned one to another with brotherly love; in honour preferring one another; Romans 12:10

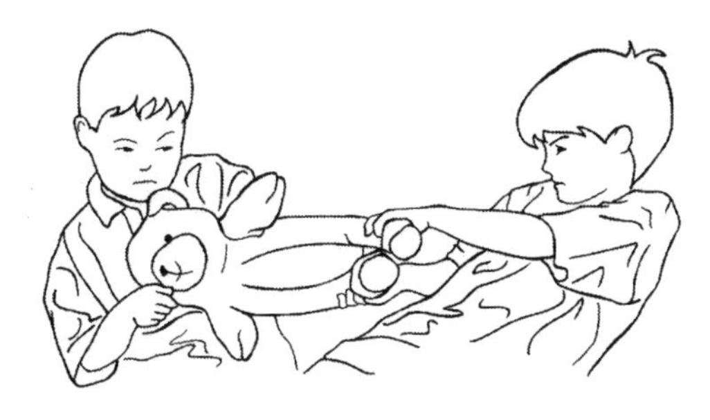

It is an honour for a man to cease from strife: but every fool will be meddling. Proverbs 20:3

God wants me to love people even when it is hard.

But I say unto you, Love your enemies, bless them that curse you, do good to them that hate you, and pray for them which despitefully use you, and persecute you; Matthew 5:44

If it be possible, as much as lieth in you, live peaceably with all men. Romans 12:18

A soft answer turneth away wrath: but grievous [harsh] words stir up anger. Proverbs 15:1

My Heavenly Father is a peacemaker. When I am a peacemaker, I am like him!

Blessed are the peacemakers: for they shall be called the children of God. Matthew 5:9

And all things are of God, who hath reconciled us to himself by Jesus Christ, and hath given to us the ministry of reconciliation; 2 Corinthians 5:18

Beloved, let us love one another: for love is of God; and every one that loveth is born of God, and knoweth God. He that loveth not knoweth not God; for God is love. 1 John 4:7-8

When God forgives me, he shows me how to forgive and be kind!

Let all bitterness, and wrath, and anger, and clamour, and evil speaking, be put away from you, with all malice: And be ye kind one to another, tenderhearted, forgiving one another, even as God for Christ's sake hath forgiven you. Ephesians 4:31-32

Let us therefore follow after the things which make for peace, and things wherewith one may edify another. Romans 14:19

God sent the flood to earth because of violence and fighting: Genesis 6:13. God hates those who love violence: Psalm 11:5.

Jesus told his disciples how to stop fighting: Luke 22:24-27.

FORGETTING

Related topic: Remember

I need God's help so I will not forget to obey!

I have gone astray like a lost sheep; Seek Your servant, For I do not forget Your commandments. Psalm 119:176

I am small and despised, Yet I do not forget Your precepts. Thy righteousness is an everlasting righteousness, and thy law is the truth. Psalm 119:141

God wants me to forget about how I have failed in the past, and work on obeying him today.

Brethren, I count not myself to have apprehended: but this one thing I do, forgetting those things which are behind, and reaching forth unto those things which are before, I press toward the mark for the prize of the high calling of God in Christ Jesus. Philippians 3:13-14

Knowing and wanting what pleases God helps me not to forget to do things that please God!

But to do good and to communicate forget not: for with such sacrifices God is well pleased. Hebrews 13:16

Be not forgetful to entertain strangers: for thereby some have entertained angels unawares. Hebrews 13:2

Doing what the Bible says helps me to remember what the Bible says.

But be ye doers of the word, and not hearers only, deceiving your own selves. For if any be a hearer of the word, and not a doer, he is like unto a man beholding his natural face in a glass: For he beholdeth himself, and goeth his way, and straightway forgetteth what manner of man he was. But whoso looketh into the perfect law of liberty, and continueth therein, he being not a forgetful hearer, but a doer of the work, this man shall be blessed in his deed. James 1:22-25

My son, forget not my law; but let thine heart keep my commandments: For length of days, and long life, and peace, shall they add to thee. Proverbs 3:1-2

That the generation to come might know them, The children who would be born, That they may arise and declare them to their children, That they may set their hope in God, And not forget the works of God, But keep His commandments; And may not be like their fathers, A stubborn and rebellious generation, A generation that did not set its heart aright, And whose spirit was not faithful to God. Psalm 78:6-8

I can remember God's work by singing songs about what he has done for me.

Bless the Lord, O my soul; And all that is within me, bless His holy name! Bless the Lord, O my soul, And forget not all His benefits: Who forgives all your iniquities, Who heals all your diseases, Who redeems your life from destruction, Who crowns you with lovingkindness and tender mercies, Who satisfies your mouth with good things, So that your youth is renewed like the eagle's. Psalm 103:1-5

Sometimes it is wise to forget small offenses against me.

The discretion of a man deferreth his anger; and it is his glory to pass over a transgression. Proverbs 19:11

God does not forget his children!

Can a woman forget her sucking [nursing] child, that she should not have compassion on the son of her womb? yea, they may forget, yet will I not forget thee. Behold, I have graven thee upon the palms of my hands; thy walls are continually before me. Isaiah 49:15-16

Pastors remind us to do right so we don't forget.

Wherefore I will not be negligent to put you always in remembrance of these things, though ye know them, and be established in the present truth. 2 Peter 1:12 (See also 2 Timothy 2:14.)

FORGIVENESS

Because God is faithful and righteous, he will forgive me when I repent from my sin.

If we confess our sins, he is faithful and just to forgive us our sins, and to cleanse us from all unrighteousness. 1 John 1:9

He hath not dealt with us after our sins; nor rewarded us according to our iniquities. For as the heaven is high above the earth, so great is his mercy toward them that fear him. As far as the east is from the west, so far hath he removed our transgressions from us. Like as a father pitieth his children, so the Lord pitieth them that fear him. Psalm 103:10-13

Jesus teaches that I cannot be right with God if I refuse to forgive others.

And when ye stand praying, forgive, if ye have ought against any: that your Father also which is in heaven may forgive you your trespasses. Mark 11:25

And be ye kind one to another, tenderhearted, forgiving one another, even as God for Christ's sake hath forgiven you. Ephesians 4:32

Jesus teaches that part of forgiving others is patience and compassion.

The servant therefore fell down, and worshipped him, saying, Lord, have patience with me, and I will pay thee all. Then the Lord of that servant was moved with compassion, and loosed him, and forgave him the debt. Matthew 18:26-27

Then came Peter to him, and said, Lord, how oft shall my brother sin against me, and I forgive him? till seven times? Jesus saith unto him, I say not unto thee, Until seven times: but, Until seventy times seven. Matthew 18:21-22

Jesus wants me to be kind when I have been mistreated.

But I say unto you, Love your enemies, bless them that curse you, do good to them that hate you, and pray for them which despitefully use you, and persecute you; Matthew 5:44

Joseph forgave his brothers. Genesis 45:4-8

FRIENDS

Related topic: Lonely

God tells me what kind of friends to look for.

He that walketh with wise men shall be wise: but a companion of fools shall be destroyed. Proverbs 13:20

I am a companion of all them that fear thee, and of them that keep thy precepts. Psalm 119:63

Make no friendship with an angry man; and with a furious man thou shalt not go: Lest thou learn his ways, and get a snare to thy soul. Proverbs 22:24-25

God tells me how to be a good friend.

He that covereth a transgression seeketh love; but he that repeateth a matter separateth very friends. Proverbs 17:9

He that blesseth his friend with a loud voice, rising early in the morning, it shall be counted a curse to him. Proverbs 27:14

True friends help each other do right!

Iron sharpeneth iron; so a man sharpeneth the countenance of his friend. Proverbs 27:17

Faithful are the wounds of a friend; but the kisses of an enemy are deceitful. Proverbs 27:6

Come and hear, all ye that fear God, and I will declare what he hath done for my soul. Psalm 66:16

True friends ask each other to pray for them.

Confess your faults one to another, and pray one for another, that ye may be healed. The effectual fervent prayer of a righteous man availeth much. James 5:16

A friend loveth at all times, and a brother is born for adversity. Proverbs 17:17

Jesus wants to be my friend! He is the best friend to have.

Greater love hath no man than this, that a man lay down his life for his friends. Ye are my friends, if ye do whatsoever I command you. Henceforth I call you not servants; for the servant knoweth not what his Lord doeth: but I have called you friends; for all things that I have heard of my Father I have made known unto you. John 15:13-15

And the scripture was fulfilled which saith, Abraham believed God, and it was imputed unto him for righteousness: and he was called the Friend of God. James 2:23

When Paul missed his friends, he was reminded to pray for them.

I thank my God upon every remembrance of you, Always in every prayer of mine for you all making request with joy, For God is my record, how greatly I long after you all in the bowels of Jesus Christ. Philippians 1:3-4, 8

I thank God, whom I serve from my forefathers with pure conscience, that without ceasing I have remembrance of thee in my prayers night and day; Greatly desiring to see thee, being mindful of thy tears, that I may be filled with joy. 2 Timothy 1:3-4

Sometimes we feel lonely when friends reject us.

My lovers and my friends stand aloof from my sore; and my kinsmen stand afar off. Psalm 38:11

At my first answer no man stood with me, but all men forsook me: I pray God that it may not be laid to their charge. 2 Timothy 4:16

Examples of friends in the Bible: Jonathan and David; Paul and Onesiphorus 2 Timothy 1:16-18; Ruth and Naomi.

Fruit of the Spirit

Related topic: Holy Spirit

The fruit of the spirit is for all Christians: girls and boys, quiet and loud, old and young!

But the fruit of the Spirit is love, joy, peace, longsuffering, gentleness, goodness, faith, Meekness, temperance: against such there is no law. Galatians 5:22-23

For the fruit of the Spirit is in all goodness and righteousness and truth; Ephesians 5:9

Now no chastening for the present seemeth to be joyous, but grievous: nevertheless afterward it yieldeth the peaceable fruit of righteousness unto them which are exercised thereby. Hebrews 12:11

Give Up

He giveth power to the faint; and to them that have no might he increaseth strength. Even the youths shall faint and be weary, and the young men shall utterly fall: But they that wait upon the Lord shall renew their strength; they shall mount up with wings as eagles; they shall run, and not be weary; and they shall walk, and not faint. Isaiah 40:29-31

I am sometimes tired of doing right, but I know God promises to reward me for not giving up.

And let us not be weary in well doing: for in due season we shall reap, if we faint not. Galatians 6:9

For God is not unrighteous to forget your work and labour of love, which ye have shewed toward his name, in that ye have ministered to the saints, and do minister. Hebrews 6:10

God promises a special blessing if I don't give up after hearing God's Word, and instead obey it!

But whoso looketh into the perfect law of liberty, and continueth therein, he being not a forgetful hearer, but a doer of the work, this man shall be blessed in his deed. James 1:25

But continue thou in the things which thou hast learned and hast been assured of, knowing of whom thou hast learned them; 2 Timothy 3:14

I can encourage my friends not to give up.

And it came to pass, when Moses held up his hand, that Israel prevailed: and when he let down his hand, Amalek prevailed. But Moses hands were heavy; and they took a stone, and put it under him, and he sat thereon; and Aaron and Hur stayed up his hands, the one on the one side, and the other on the other side; and his hands were steady until the going down of the sun. And Joshua discomfited Amalek and his people with the edge of the sword. Exodus 17:11-13

God helps me not give up when I have failed, and I can have courage to start doing right again.

For a just man falleth seven times, and riseth up again: but the wicked shall fall into mischief. Proverbs 24:16

I am encouraged by remembering how Jesus did not give up at the cross.

Wherefore seeing we also are compassed about with so great a cloud of witnesses, let us lay aside every weight, and the sin which doth so easily beset us, and let us run with patience the race that is set before us, Looking unto Jesus the author and finisher of our faith; who for the joy that was set before him endured the cross, despising the shame, and is set down at the right hand of the throne of God.
Hebrews 12:1-2

For consider him that endured such contradiction of sinners against himself, lest ye be wearied and faint in your minds.
Hebrews 12:3

God wants me to give up sin!

The desire accomplished is sweet to the soul: but it is abomination to fools to depart from evil. Proverbs 13:19

> Elijah was in danger and felt all alone when he wanted to give up. God encouraged him in 1 Kings 19.
>
> Jonah was angry when God forgave people he hated. His anger caused him to want to give up. Jonah 4.

GIVING

God wants me to give happily.

Every man according as he purposeth in his heart, so let him give; not grudgingly, or of necessity: for God loveth a cheerful giver. 2 Corinthians 9:7

God wants me to give to please Him, not to impress others!

Take heed that ye do not your alms before men, to be seen of them: otherwise ye have no reward of your Father which is in heaven. Therefore when thou doest thine alms, do not sound a trumpet before thee, as the hypocrites do in the synagogues and in the streets, that they may have glory of men. Verily I say unto you, They have their reward. But when thou doest alms, let not thy left hand know what thy right hand doeth: That thine alms may be in secret: and thy Father which seeth in secret himself shall reward thee openly. Matthew 6:1-4

God does not want me to give money if I do not have it.

For if there be first a willing mind [to give], it is accepted according to that a man hath, and not according to that he hath not. 2 Corinthians 8:12

I cannot please God by giving without loving.

And though I bestow all my goods to feed the poor, and though I give my body to be burned, and have not charity, it profiteth me nothing. 1 Corinthians 13:3

The people were so happy to be helping build the tabernacle that Moses had to tell them to stop bringing things when they had enough! Exodus 36:1-7

Jesus loves to use little things in his plans! Proverbs 30:24-28, 1 Corinthians 1:26-28

God

Related topics: Omniscience, Omnipotence, Knowing God

God is good.

As for God, his way is perfect: the word of the Lord is tried: he is a buckler [shield] to all those that trust in him. Psalm 18:30

I had fainted, unless I had believed to see the goodness of the LORD in the land of the living. Wait on the LORD: be of good courage, and he shall strengthen thine heart: wait, I say, on the LORD. Psalm 27:13-14

God is faithful.

Know therefore that the Lord thy God, he is God, the faithful God, which keepeth covenant and mercy with them that love him and keep his commandments to a thousand generations; Deuteronomy 7:9

I will sing of the mercies of the Lord for ever: with my mouth will I make known thy faithfulness to all generations. Psalm 89:1

It is of the Lord's mercies that we are not consumed, because his compassions fail not. They are new every morning: great is thy faithfulness. Lamentations 3:22,23

God is love.

The Lord hath appeared of old unto me, saying, Yea, I have loved thee with an everlasting love: therefore with lovingkindness have I drawn thee. Jeremiah 31:3

For God so loved the world, that he gave his only begotten Son, that whosoever believeth in him should not perish, but have everlasting life. John 3:16

How excellent is thy lovingkindness, O God! Therefore the children of men put their trust under the shadow of thy wings. Psalm 36:7

Going to Church

God's church is very important to him!

But if I tarry long, that thou mayest know how thou oughtest to behave thyself in the house of God, which is the church of the living God, the pillar and ground of the truth.
1 Timothy 3:15

God's children like going to church.

I was glad when they said unto me, Let us go into the house of the Lord. Psalm 122:1

For a day in thy courts is better than a thousand. I had rather be a doorkeeper in the house of my God, than to dwell in the tents of wickedness. Psalm 84:10

Thy words were found, and I did eat them; and thy word was unto me the joy and rejoicing of mine heart: for I am called by thy name, O Lord God of hosts. Jeremiah 15:16

God's children learn God's ways at church.

Gather the people together, men, and women, and children, and thy stranger that is within thy gates, that they may hear, and that they may learn, and fear the Lord your God, and observe to do all the words of this law: Deuteronomy 31:12

For I was envious at the foolish, when I saw the prosperity of the wicked. Until I went into the sanctuary of God; then understood I their end. Psalm 73:3, 17

God's children help other Christians at church.

And let us consider one another to provoke unto love and to good works: Not forsaking the assembling of ourselves together, as the manner of some is; but exhorting one another: and so much the more, as ye see the day approaching.
Hebrews 10:24-25

Gospel

Related topics: Jesus, Salvation, Repentance

Gospel means "good news." In the Bible, the gospel means the story of Jesus. (See Jesus.)

And the angel said unto them, Fear not: for, behold, I bring you good tidings of great joy, which shall be to all people. For unto you is born this day in the city of David a Saviour, which is Christ the Lord. Luke 2:10-11

The Spirit of the Lord GOD is upon me; because the LORD hath anointed me to preach good tidings unto the meek; he hath sent me to bind up the brokenhearted, to proclaim liberty to the captives, and the opening of the prison to them that are bound; Isaiah 61:1 (Jesus said this verse was talking about him! See Luke 4:16-21)

The gospel tells me about Jesus' birth, death, and resurrection. (See Salvation.)

Moreover, brethren, I declare unto you the gospel which I preached unto you... For I delivered unto you first of all that which I also received, how that Christ died for our sins according to the scriptures; And that he was buried, and that he rose again the third day according to the scriptures: 1 Corinthians 15:1a, 3-4

But God, who is rich in mercy, for his great love wherewith he loved us, Even when we were dead in sins, hath quickened us together with Christ, (by grace ye are saved;) And hath raised us up together, and made us sit together in heavenly places in Christ Jesus: That in the ages to come he might shew the exceeding riches of his grace in his kindness toward us through Christ Jesus. Ephesians 2:4-7 (Verses 8 and 9 can be found in the Salvation topic.)

The gospel tells me about salvation. (See Salvation.)

And saying, The time is fulfilled, and the kingdom of God is at hand: repent ye, and believe the gospel. Mark 1:15

For I am not ashamed of the gospel of Christ: for it is the power of God unto salvation to every one that believeth; to the Jew first, and also to the Greek. Romans 1:16

But they have not all obeyed the gospel. For Esaias saith, Lord, who hath believed our report? So then faith cometh by hearing, and hearing by the word of God. Romans 10:16-17

God wants me to tell people the gospel of Jesus and share my life with them. (See Evangelism.)
And he said unto them, Go ye into all the world, and preach the gospel to every creature. Mark 16:15

So being affectionately desirous of you, we were willing to have imparted unto you, not the gospel of God only, but also our own souls, because ye were dear unto us.
1 Thessalonians 2:8

HAPPY

Knowing and obeying God and his word will make me happy!
If ye know these things, happy are ye if ye do them.
John 13:17

I rejoice at thy word, as one that findeth great spoil.
Psalm 119:162

I will sing unto the Lord as long as I live: I will sing praise to my God while I have my being. My meditation of him shall be sweet: I will be glad in the Lord. Psalm 104:33-34

Thy testimonies have I taken as an heritage for ever: for they are the rejoicing of my heart. Psalm 119:111

Delight thyself also in the Lord; and he shall give thee the desires of thine heart. Psalm 37:4

I delight to do thy will, O my God: yea, thy law is within my heart. Psalm 40:8

A
B
C
D
E
F
G
H
I
J
K
L
M
N
O
P
Q
R
S
T
U
V
W
X
Y
Z

Helping others makes me happy!

He that despiseth his neighbour sinneth: but he that hath mercy on the poor, happy is he. Proverbs 14:21

Learning to be wise makes me happy!

Happy is the man that findeth wisdom, and the man that getteth understanding. Proverbs 3:13

Trusting in God makes me happy!

He that handleth a matter wisely shall find good: and whoso trusteth in the Lord, happy is he. Proverbs 16:20

O taste and see that the Lord is good: blessed is the man that trusteth in thee. Psalm 34:8

When God forgives me, I am happy and want to shout for joy!

Blessed [Happy] is he whose transgression is forgiven, whose sin is covered. Blessed is the man unto whom the Lord imputeth not iniquity, and in whose spirit there is no guile. When I kept silence, my bones waxed old through my roaring all the day long. I acknowledged my sin unto thee, and mine iniquity have I not hid. I said, I will confess my transgressions unto the Lord; and thou forgavest the iniquity of my sin. Selah. Be glad in the Lord, and rejoice, ye righteous: and shout for joy, all ye that are upright in heart. Psalm 32:1-3, 5, 11

Jehoshaphat made God his delight.

Now the Lord was with Jehoshaphat, because he walked in the former ways of his father David; he did not seek the Baals, but sought the God of his father, and walked in His commandments and not according to the acts of Israel. Therefore the Lord established the kingdom in his hand; and all Judah gave presents to Jehoshaphat, and he had riches and honor in abundance. And his heart took delight in the ways of the Lord; moreover he removed the high places and wooden images from Judah. 2 Chronicles 17:3-6

God tells me what makes HIM happy!

He does not delight in the strength of the horse; He takes no pleasure in the legs of a man. The Lord takes pleasure in those who fear Him, In those who hope in His mercy. Psalm 147:10-11

Lying lips are abomination to the Lord: but they that deal truly are his delight. Proverbs 12:22

The sacrifice of the wicked is an abomination to the Lord: but the prayer of the upright is his delight. Proverbs 15:8

They that are of a froward [stubbornly disobedient] heart are abomination to the Lord: but such as are upright in their way are his delight. Proverbs 11:20

Heaven

Nobody will cry in heaven; nobody will be sad in heaven; nobody will die or hurt in heaven!

And God shall wipe away all tears from their eyes; and there shall be no more death, neither sorrow, nor crying, neither shall there be any more pain: for the former things are passed away. Revelation 21:4

God tells his children what heaven is like: heaven doesn't have a sun or moon. Heaven doesn't have a church building! Heaven is a happy, beautiful place.

And the city had no need of the sun, neither of the moon to shine in it: for the glory of God did lighten it, and the Lamb is the light thereof. Revelation 21:23

And I saw no temple therein: for the Lord God Almighty and the Lamb are the temple of it. Revelation 21:22

God's children will eat food in heaven, including fruit from a tree that has a different kind of fruit each month.

And he shewed me a pure river of water of life, clear as crystal, proceeding out of the throne of God and of the Lamb. In the midst of the street of it, and on either side of the river, was there the tree of life which bare twelve manner of fruits, and yielded her fruit every month: and the leaves of the tree were for the healing of the nations. Revelation 22:1-2

God promises a special blessing to his children who are excited and looking forward to being in heaven with Jesus.

Henceforth there is laid up for me a crown of righteousness, which the Lord, the righteous judge, shall give me at that day: and not to me only, but unto all them also that love his appearing. 2 Timothy 4:8

Let not your heart be troubled: ye believe in God, believe also in me. In my Father's house are many mansions: if it were not so, I would have told you. I go to prepare a place for you. And if I go and prepare a place for you, I will come again, and receive you unto myself; that where I am, there ye may be also. John 14:1-3

God's children look forward to heaven, but they also are happy to serve God on earth!

For I am in a strait betwixt two, having a desire to depart, and to be with Christ; which is far better: Philippians 1:23

Holy Spirit

The Holy Spirit gives me spiritual life!

Jesus answered, Verily, verily, I say unto thee, Except a man be born of water and of the Spirit, he cannot enter into the kingdom of God. That which is born of the flesh is flesh; and that which is born of the Spirit is spirit. John 3:5-6

The Holy Spirit comforts me when I am sad.

And I will pray the Father, and he shall give you another Comforter, that he may abide with you for ever; Even the Spirit of truth; whom the world cannot receive, because it seeth him not, neither knoweth him: but ye know him; for he dwelleth with you, and shall be in you. John 14:16-17

The Holy Spirit helps me learn and understand the Bible.

I have yet many things to say unto you, but ye cannot bear them now. Howbeit when he, the Spirit of truth, is come, he will guide you into all truth: for he shall not speak of himself; but whatsoever he shall hear, that shall he speak: and he will shew you things to come. John 16:12-13

Sanctify them through thy truth: thy word is truth. John 17:17

And take the helmet of salvation, and the sword of the Spirit, which is the word of God: Ephesians 6:17

The Holy Spirit prays for me when I cannot think of the words to say!

Likewise the Spirit also helpeth our infirmities: for we know not what we should pray for as we ought: but the Spirit itself maketh intercession for us with groanings which cannot be uttered. And he that searcheth the hearts knoweth what is the mind of the Spirit, because he maketh intercession for the saints according to the will of God. Romans 8:26-27

Hope

For thou art my hope, O Lord God: thou art my trust from my youth. Psalm 71:5

May the God of hope fill you with all joy and peace in believing, so that by the power of the Holy Spirit you may abound in hope. Romans 15:13

Because God is good and all powerful, I have hope.

Behold, the eye of the Lord is upon them that fear him, upon them that hope in his mercy. Psalm 33:18

Why art thou cast down, O my soul? and why art thou disquieted in me? hope thou in God: for I shall yet praise him for the help of his countenance. Psalm 42:5

My soul, wait thou only upon God; for my expectation [hope] is from him. He only is my rock and my salvation: he is my defence; I shall not be moved. In God is my salvation and my glory: the rock of my strength, and my refuge, is in God. Trust in him at all times; ye people, pour out your heart before him: God is a refuge for us. Selah. Psalm 62:5-8

I am reminded to hope when I read about God in the Bible.

I wait for the Lord, my soul doth wait, and in his word do I hope. Psalm 130:5

Happy is he that hath the God of Jacob for his help, whose hope is in the Lord his God: Psalm 146:5

For whatsoever things were written aforetime were written for our learning, that we through patience and comfort of the scriptures might have hope. Romans 15:4

God is happy when I hope and trust in his care for me.

The Lord taketh pleasure in them that fear him, in those that hope in his mercy. Psalm 147:11

It is of the Lord's mercies that we are not consumed, because his compassions fail not. They are new every morning: great is thy faithfulness. The Lord is my portion, saith my soul; therefore will I hope in him. The Lord is good unto them that wait for him, to the soul that seeketh him. It is good that a man should both hope and quietly wait for the salvation of the Lord. Lamentations 3:21-24

Rejoicing in hope; patient in tribulation; continuing instant in prayer; Romans 12:12

For therefore we both labour and suffer reproach, because we trust in the living God, who is the Saviour of all men, specially of those that believe. 1 Timothy 4:10

Horses

God uses horses to teach me what he is like.

The horse is prepared against the day of battle: but safety is of the Lord. Proverbs 21:31

Some trust in chariots, and some in horses: but we will remember the name of the Lord our God. Psalm 20:7

I will instruct thee and teach thee in the way which thou shalt go: I will guide thee with mine eye. Be ye not as the horse, or as the mule, which have no understanding: whose mouth must be held in with bit and bridle, lest they come near unto thee. Psalm 32:8-9

Woe to them that go down to Egypt for help; and stay on horses, and trust in chariots, because they are many; and in horsemen, because they are very strong; but they look not unto the Holy One of Israel, neither seek the Lord!
Isaiah 31:1

He delighteth not in the strength of the horse: he taketh not pleasure in the legs of a man. The Lord taketh pleasure in them that fear him, in those that hope in his mercy.
Psalm 147:10-11

Hast thou given the horse strength?
Hast thou clothed his neck with thunder?
Canst thou make him afraid as a grasshopper?
The glory of his nostrils is terrible.
He paweth in the valley, and rejoiceth in his strength:
He goeth on to meet the armed men.
He mocketh at fear, and is not affrighted;
Neither turneth he back from the sword.
The quiver rattleth against him,
The glittering spear and the shield.
Job 39:19-23

There is no king saved by the multitude of an host: a mighty man is not delivered by much strength. An horse is a vain thing for safety: neither shall he deliver any by his great strength. Behold, the eye of the Lord is upon them that fear him, upon them that hope in his mercy; Psalm 33:16-18

And I saw heaven opened, and behold a white horse; and he that sat upon him was called Faithful and True, and in righteousness he doth judge and make war. His eyes were as a flame of fire, and on his head were many crowns; and he had a name written, that no man knew, but he himself. Revelation 19:11-12

A B C D E F G H I J K L M N O P Q R S T U V W X Y Z

HUMILITY

Related topics: Pride, Fair, Anger

He hath shewed thee, O man, what is good; and what doth the Lord require of thee, but to do justly, and to love mercy, and to walk humbly with thy God? Micah 6:8

Likewise, ye younger, submit yourselves unto the elder. Yea, all of you be subject one to another, and be clothed with humility: for God resisteth the proud, and giveth grace to the humble. 1 Peter 5:5

A humble child will not insist on his own way, or become angry when life doesn't seem fair. When he learns to be meek, he will have peace!

Rest in the Lord, and wait patiently for him: fret not thyself because of him who prospereth in his way, because of the man who bringeth wicked devices to pass. Cease from anger, and forsake wrath: fret not thyself in any wise to do evil. But the meek shall inherit the earth; and shall delight themselves in the abundance of peace. Psalm 37: 7-8, 11

Children learn to be humble when they give others the best choice.

Let nothing be done through strife or vainglory; but in lowliness of mind let each esteem other better than themselves. Look not every man on his own things, but every man also on the things of others. Philippians 2:3-4

God wants his children to be humble like Jesus.

Let this mind be in you, which was also in Christ Jesus: Who, being in the form of God, thought it not robbery to be equal with God: But made himself of no reputation, and took upon him the form of a servant, and was made in the likeness of men: And being found in fashion as a man, he humbled himself, and became obedient unto death, even the death of the cross. Philippians 2:5-8

Whosoever therefore shall humble himself as this little child, the same is greatest in the kingdom of heaven. Matthew 18:4

Moses was the meekest man on the earth (Numbers 12:3). He was more concerned about others and God's glory than about his own power and success. Numbers 14:11-20

Jesus

Related topics: God, Holy Spirit

Jesus came to earth so that I could know God, love him, and be his friend!

And we know that the Son of God is come, and hath given us an understanding, that we may know him that is true, and we are in him that is true, even in his Son Jesus Christ. This is the true God, and eternal life. 1 John 5:20

For unto us a child is born, unto us a son is given: and the government shall be upon his shoulder: and his name shall be called Wonderful, Counsellor, The mighty God, The everlasting Father, The Prince of Peace. Isaiah 9:6

This is my commandment, That ye love one another, as I have loved you. Greater love hath no man than this, that a man lay down his life for his friends. Ye are my friends, if ye do whatsoever I command you. John 15:12-14

Peace I leave with you, my peace I give unto you: not as the world giveth, give I unto you. Let not your heart be troubled, neither let it be afraid. John 14:27

Jesus is the only way to make peace with God.

Jesus saith unto him, I am the way, the truth, and the life: no man cometh unto the Father, but by me. John 14:6

For when we were yet without strength, in due time Christ died for the ungodly. For scarcely for a righteous man will one die: yet peradventure for a good man some would even dare to die. But God commendeth his love toward us, in that, while we were yet sinners, Christ died for us. Much more then, being now justified by his blood, we shall be saved from wrath through him. Romans 5:6-9

When Jesus said he was God, some Jews who did not like his words tried to kill him.

[Jesus said:] I and my Father are one. Then the Jews took up stones again to stone him. Jesus answered them, Many good works have I shewed you from my Father; for which of those works do ye stone me? The Jews answered him, saying, For a good work we stone thee not; but for blasphemy; and because that thou, being a man, makest thyself God. John 10:30-33

Therefore the Jews sought the more to kill him, because he not only had broken the sabbath, but said also that God was his Father, making himself equal with God. John 5:18

Jesus said unto them, Verily, verily, I say unto you, Before Abraham was, I am. Then took they up stones to cast at him: but Jesus hid himself, and went out of the temple, going through the midst of them, and so passed by. John 8:58-59 (Compare with Exodus 3:14: "I AM.")

The Bible also shows that Jesus is God when Jesus does things that only God can do.

When Jesus saw their faith, he said unto the sick of the palsy, Son, thy sins be forgiven thee. But there were certain of the scribes sitting there, and reasoning in their hearts, Why doth this man thus speak blasphemies? who can forgive sins but God only? Mark 2:5-7 (Compare with Isaiah 55:6-7 and Psalm 32:1-2.)

All things were made by him; and without him was not any thing made that was made. John 1:3 (Also see the story of Jesus creating fish and bread in Mark 6:38-44. Compare with Isaiah 40:28)

Jesus answered and said unto them, Go and shew John again those things which ye do hear and see: The blind receive their sight, and the lame walk, the lepers are cleansed, and the deaf hear, the dead are raised up, and the poor have the gospel preached to them. Matthew 11:4-5 (Compare with Isaiah 35:4-8.)

Jesus' birth (Matthew 1:18–2:23 and Luke 1:26–2:22)

When Jesus was a boy (Luke 2:40-52)

Jesus talking about children (Matthew 18:1-6, 10; 19:13-24)

Jesus prayed for me! (All of John 17, especially verse 20)

Jesus' death, burial, and resurrection (Matthew 26:47–28:20; Mark 14:43–16:20; Luke 22:47–24:53; John 18–21)

KINDNESS

Related topic: Love

One way I can be kind is to forgive others for Jesus' sake, the same way God forgave me!

And be ye kind one to another, tenderhearted, forgiving one another, even as God for Christ's sake hath forgiven you. Ephesians 4:32

Another way I can be kind is to be patient, and learn to love others.

Charity [love] suffereth long, and is kind; charity envieth not; charity vaunteth not itself, is not puffed up, Doth not behave itself unseemly, seeketh not her own, is not easily provoked, thinketh no evil; 1 Corinthians 13:4-5

But whoso hath this world's good, and seeth his brother have need, and shutteth up his bowels of compassion from him, how dwelleth the love of God in him? My little children, let us not love in word, neither in tongue; but in deed and in truth. 1 John 3:17-18

When I am kind to younger children, or people who seem unimportant, Jesus tells me it's like I'm being kind to HIM!

Then shall the righteous answer him, saying, Lord, when saw we thee an hungred, and fed thee? or thirsty, and gave thee drink? When saw we thee a stranger, and took thee in? or naked, and clothed thee? Or when saw we thee sick, or in prison, and came unto thee? And the King shall answer and say unto them, Verily I say unto you, Inasmuch as ye have done it unto one of the least of these my brethren, ye have done it unto me. Matthew 25:37-40

God wants me to be kind to my friends and enemies even when they are not being kind back.

But love ye your enemies, and do good, and lend, hoping for nothing again; and your reward shall be great, and ye shall be the children of the Highest: for he is kind unto the unthankful and to the evil. Luke 6:35

I can be kind by encouraging my friends who are sad.

Heaviness in the heart of man maketh it stoop: but a good word maketh it glad. Proverbs 12:25

God wants me to enjoy thinking ahead and planning ways to be kind.

Do they not err that devise evil? but mercy and truth shall be to them that devise good. Proverbs 14:22

As we have therefore opportunity, let us do good unto all men, especially unto them who are of the household of faith. Galatians 6:10

Knowing God

God wants me to try to know him, to look for him.

But seek ye first the kingdom of God, and his righteousness; and all these things shall be added unto you. Matthew 6:33

And ye shall seek me, and find me, when ye shall search for me with all your heart. Jeremiah 29:13

And they that know thy name will put their trust in thee: for thou, Lord, hast not forsaken them that seek thee. Psalm 9:10

Draw nigh to God, and he will draw nigh to you. Cleanse your hands, ye sinners; and purify your hearts, ye double minded. James 4:8

Let all those that seek thee rejoice and be glad in thee: let such as love thy salvation say continually, The Lord be magnified. Psalm 40:16

God gives me the desire to know him.

O God, thou art my God; early will I seek thee: my soul thirsteth for thee, my flesh longeth for thee in a dry thirsty land, where no water is; To see thy power and thy glory, so as I have seen thee in the sanctuary. Because thy lovingkindness is better than life, my lips shall praise thee. Psalm 63:1-3

My soul longeth, yea, even fainteth for the courts of the Lord: my heart and my flesh crieth out for the living God. Psalm 84:2

As the hart [deer] panteth after the water brooks, so panteth my soul after thee, O God. My soul thirsteth for God, for the living God: when shall I come and appear before God? My tears have been my meat day and night, while they continually say unto me, Where is thy God? When I remember these things, I pour out my soul in me: for I had gone with the multitude, I went with them to the house of God, with the voice of joy and praise, with a multitude that kept holyday. Psalm 42:1-4

God is delighted when I want to know him.

But grow in grace, and in the knowledge of our Lord and Saviour Jesus Christ. To him be glory both now and for ever. Amen. 2 Peter 3:18

Thus saith the Lord, Let not the wise man glory in his wisdom, neither let the mighty man glory in his might, let not the rich man glory in his riches: But let him that glorieth glory in this, that he understandeth and knoweth me, that I am the Lord which exercise lovingkindness, judgment, and righteousness, in the earth: for in these things I delight, saith the Lord. Jeremiah 9:23-24

> Isaiah 40 is a whole chapter about our wonderful God.
>
> King David wrote Psalms that show what it looks like to know God.
>
> Paul told the church at Philippi that one of his biggest goals was to know God better. Philippians 3:10

Lazy

See Work.

Learning Problems

See Disability.

Listening

When Jesus was a boy, he listened and asked questions.

And it came to pass, that after three days they found him [Jesus] in the temple, sitting in the midst of the doctors, both hearing them, and asking them questions. Luke 2:46

God's children learn to listen to and follow Jesus.

My sheep hear my voice, and I know them, and they follow me: John 10:27

A foolish child is more interested in his own opinions than listening.

A fool hath no delight in understanding, but that his heart may discover itself. Proverbs 18:2

He that answereth a matter before he heareth it, it is folly and shame unto him. Proverbs 18:13

Listening is one way I can learn to control my anger.

Wherefore, my beloved brethren, let every man be swift to hear, slow to speak, slow to wrath: James 1:19

Listening to truth will help me to become wise.

Hear counsel, and receive instruction, that thou mayest be wise in thy latter end.
Proverbs 19:20

Now therefore hearken unto me [wisdom], O ye children: for blessed are they that keep my ways. Hear instruction, and be wise, and refuse it not. Blessed is the man that heareth me, watching daily at my gates, waiting at the posts of my doors. Proverbs 8:32-34

The way of a fool is right in his own eyes: but he that hearkeneth unto counsel is wise. Proverbs 12:15

Read a good example of Samuel, who listened well when he was a child, in 1 Samuel 3.

Mary listened with a believing heart when Gabriel told her she would give birth to Jesus. She wrote a poem about it. Luke 1:34-38, and Luke 1:46-55

Zacharias listened with an unbelieving heart when Gabriel told him that his wife would give birth. Luke 1:18-20

Lonely

Related topic: Friends

God is my helper and friend when I am lonely.

For he hath said, I will never leave thee, nor forsake thee. So that we may boldly say, The Lord is my helper, and I will not fear what man shall do unto me. Hebrews 13:5b-6

I looked on my right hand, and beheld, but there was no man that would know me: refuge failed me; no man cared for my soul. I cried unto thee, O Lord: I said, Thou art my refuge and my portion in the land of the living. Psalm 142:4-5

Help, Lord; for the godly man ceaseth; for the faithful fail from among the children of men. They speak vanity every one with his neighbour: with flattering lips and with a double heart do they speak Psalm 12:1-2

King David wrote poems of his prayers when he was lonely.

Hear my prayer, O Lord, and let my cry come unto thee. Hide not thy face from me in the day when I am in trouble; incline thine ear unto me: in the day when I call answer me speedily. For my days are consumed like smoke, and my bones are burned as an hearth. My heart is smitten, and withered like grass; so that I forget to eat my bread. By reason of the voice of my groaning my bones cleave to my skin. I am like a pelican of the wilderness: I am like an owl of the desert. I watch, and am as a sparrow alone upon the house top. Psalm 102:1-7

Jesus wants to be my friend.

Greater love hath no man than this, that a man lay down his life for his friends. Ye are my friends, if ye do whatsoever I command you. Henceforth I call you not servants; for the servant knoweth not what his Lord doeth: but I have called you friends; for all things that I have heard of my Father I have made known unto you. John 15:13-15

God showed me how to find someone who needs a friend.

Greater love hath no man than this, that a man lay down his life for his friends. John 15:13

When I feel alone, God wants me to come close to him and ask him for help.

Whom have I in heaven but thee? and there is none upon earth that I desire beside thee. My flesh and my heart faileth: but God is the strength of my heart, and my portion for ever. But it is good for me to draw near to God: I have put my trust in the Lord God, that I may declare all thy works. Psalm 73:25-26, 28

God will always supply my needs, even though there may be times when I do not have a close friend.

And the Lord God said, It is not good that the man should be alone; I will make him an help meet for him. Genesis 2:18

But my God shall supply all your need according to his riches in glory by Christ Jesus. Philippians 4:19

For the Lord God is a sun and shield: the Lord will give grace and glory: no good thing will he withhold from them that walk uprightly. O Lord of hosts, blessed is the man that trusteth in thee. Psalm 84:11-12

Being lonely reminds me that I live for God, and he never forgets my work for him!

Therefore, my beloved brethren, be ye steadfast, unmoveable, always abounding in the work of the Lord, forasmuch as ye know that your labour is not in vain in the Lord. 1 Corinthians 15:58

I am never truly alone.

If I take the wings of the morning, and dwell in the uttermost parts of the sea; Even there shall thy hand lead me, and thy right hand shall hold me. Psalm 139:9-10

LOVE

Related topic: God

God's love sets the example for me to follow.

Beloved, let us love one another: for love is of God; and every one that loveth is born of God, and knoweth God. He that loveth not knoweth not God; for God is love.
1 John 4:7-8

Hereby perceive we the love of God, because he laid down his life for us: and we ought to lay down our lives for the brethren. 1 John 3:16

Beloved, if God so loved us, we ought also to love one another. 1 John 4:11

God wants me to learn how to love him!

Take good heed therefore unto yourselves, that ye love the Lord your God. Joshua 23:11

We love him, because he first loved us. 1 John 4:19

And now, Israel, what doth the Lord thy God require of thee, but to fear the Lord thy God, to walk in all his ways, and to love him, and to serve the Lord thy God with all thy heart and with all thy soul, Deuteronomy 10:12

Love is not just a feeling or something I say; love is something I DO!

My little children, let us not love in word, neither in tongue; but in deed and in truth. 1 John 3:18

I can love others by overlooking faults.

A friend loveth at all times, and a brother is born for adversity. Proverbs 17:17

Hatred stirreth up strifes: but love covereth all sins.
Proverbs 10:12

And above all things have fervent charity among yourselves: for charity shall cover the multitude of sins. 1 Peter 4:8

I can love by choosing what is best for others.

Love worketh no ill to his neighbour: therefore love is the fulfilling of the law. Romans 13:10

Be kindly affectioned one to another with brotherly love; in honour preferring one another; Not slothful in business; fervent in spirit; serving the Lord; Rejoicing in hope; patient in tribulation; continuing instant in prayer; Distributing to the necessity of saints; given to hospitality. Romans 12:9-13

The whole chapter of 1 Corinthians 13 is about love.

Love suffers long.	See Patient
Love is kind.	See Kindness
Love does not envy.	See Envy/ Jealousy
Love does not puff itself up.	See Humility and Pride
Love does not behave unseemly.	See Modest
Love does not seek her own.	See Selfishness
Love is not easily provoked.	See Anger
Love thinks no evil.	See Hope
Love rejoices in truth.	See Truth

LYING

Related topic: Truth Telling

God hates lying.

Lying lips are abomination to the Lord: but they that deal truly are his delight. Proverbs 12:22

King David prayed that people would stop lying.

Let the lying lips be put to silence; which speak grievous things proudly and contemptuously against the righteous. Psalm 31:18

I want God to help me love truth and hate lying.

I hate and abhor lying: but thy law do I love. Psalm 119:163

Let not mercy and truth forsake thee: bind them about thy neck; write them upon the table of thine heart: Proverbs 3:3

Putting away lying, speak every man truth with his neighbor: Ephesians 4:25

Keep thy tongue from evil, and thy lips from speaking guile. Psalm 34:13

Achan stole, and then he lied about what he had done. Joshua 7:10-26

Mean People

Related topics: Enemies, Fighting, Forgiveness

When I am mean

See that none render evil for evil unto any man; but ever follow that which is good, both among yourselves, and to all men. 1 Thessalonians 5:15

When others are mean

Rejoice not when thine enemy falleth, and let not thine heart be glad when he stumbleth: Lest the Lord see it, and it displease him, and he turn away his wrath from him. Proverbs 24:17-18

Fret not thyself because of evil men, neither be thou envious at the wicked: For there shall be no reward to the evil man; the candle of the wicked shall be put out. Proverbs 24:19-20

If thine enemy be hungry, give him bread to eat; and if he be thirsty, give him water to drink: For thou shalt heap coals of fire upon his head, and the Lord shall reward thee. Proverbs 25:21-22

God will avenge wrong things in his time.

Dearly beloved, avenge not yourselves, but rather give place unto wrath: for it is written, Vengeance is mine; I will repay, saith the Lord. Therefore if thine enemy hunger, feed him; if he thirst, give him drink: for in so doing thou shalt heap coals of fire on his head. Be not overcome of evil, but overcome evil with good. Romans 12:19-21

God wants me to stand up to bullies for others who cannot defend themselves.

Learn to do well; seek judgment, relieve the oppressed, judge the fatherless, plead for the widow. Isaiah 1:17

God wants me to help those having a hard time.

Now we exhort you, brethren, warn them that are unruly, comfort the feebleminded, support the weak, be patient toward all men. 1 Thessalonians 5:14

> King David wrote songs when he was troubled with people. See Psalms 35, 56, 57, and 61.
>
> Paul was a mean person until God changed his heart. Read about it starting in Acts 9.

Modesty

Related topic: Humility

Modesty starts with humble and pure thoughts.

Keep thy heart with all diligence; for out of it are the issues of life. Proverbs 4:23

Whose adorning let it not be that outward adorning of plaiting the hair, and of wearing of gold, or of putting on of apparel; But let it be the hidden man of the heart, in that which is not corruptible, even the ornament of a meek and quiet spirit, which is in the sight of God of great price.
1 Peter 3:3-4

What? know ye not that your body is the temple of the Holy Ghost which is in you, which ye have of God, and ye are not your own? For ye are bought with a price: therefore glorify God in your body, and in your spirit, which are God's.
1 Corinthians 6:19-20

Modesty results in actions, words, and even clothing chosen to please God, and build up others.

He hath shewed thee, O man, what is good; and what doth the Lord require of thee, but to do justly, and to love mercy, and to walk humbly [modestly] with thy God? Micah 6:8

Whether therefore ye eat, or drink, or whatsoever ye do, do all to the glory of God. 1 Corinthians 10:31

Let us therefore follow after the things which make for peace, and things wherewith one may edify another. Romans 14:19

God want me to dress and act in a way that doesn't show off.

In like manner also, that women adorn themselves in modest apparel, with shamefacedness and sobriety; not with broided hair, or gold, or pearls, or costly array; But (which becometh women professing godliness) with good works.
1 Timothy 2:9-10

Thus saith the Lord, Let not the wise man glory [boast] in his wisdom, neither let the mighty man glory in his might, let not the rich man glory in his riches: But let him that glorieth glory in this, that he understandeth and knoweth me, that I am the Lord which exercise lovingkindness, judgment, and righteousness, in the earth: for in these things I delight, saith the Lord. Jeremiah 9:23-24

MONEY

Related topics: Giving, Contentment

Labour not to be rich: cease from thine own wisdom. Proverbs 23:4

But godliness with contentment is great gain. 1 Timothy 6:6

[Wisdom] is more precious than rubies: and all the things thou canst desire are not to be compared unto her. Proverbs 3:15

God wants me to use money to help others.

Charge them that are rich in this world, that they be not high-minded, nor trust in uncertain riches, but in the living God, who giveth us richly all things to enjoy; 1 Timothy 6:17

That they do good, that they be rich in good works, ready to distribute, willing to communicate [share]; 1 Timothy 6:18

He that trusteth in his riches shall fall; but the righteous shall flourish as a branch. Proverbs 11:28

Having a poor, happy home is better than a rich, fighting home.

Better is little with the fear of the Lord than great treasure and trouble therewith. Better is a dinner of herbs where love is, than a stalled ox and hatred therewith. Proverbs 15:16-17

The most important things in my life cannot be bought with money.

And he [Jesus] said unto them, Take heed, and beware of covetousness: for a man's life consisteth not in the abundance of the things which he possesseth. Luke 12:15

OBEDIENCE

Children obey your parents in the Lord, for this is right. Ephesians 6:1

And the people said unto Joshua, The Lord our God will we serve, and his voice will we obey. Joshua 24:24

I thought on my ways, and turned my feet unto thy testimonies. I made haste, and delayed not to keep thy commandments. Psalm 119:59-60

Jesus was a good example as a boy. He obeyed his parents, even they didn't understand him!

And they understood not the saying which he spake unto them. And he went down with them, and came to Nazareth, and was subject unto them: but his mother kept all these sayings in her heart. Luke 2:50-51

God wants me to obey other authorities, too.

Put them in mind to be subject to principalities and powers, to obey magistrates, to be ready to every good work, to speak evil of no man, to be no brawlers, but gentle, shewing all meekness unto all men. Titus 3:1-2

Obey them that have the rule over you, and submit yourselves: for they watch for your souls, as they that must give account, that they may do it with joy, and not with grief: for that is unprofitable for you. Hebrews 13:17

OMNIPOTENT

God can do anything he wants to do.

For with God nothing shall be impossible. Luke 1:37

Ah Lord God! behold, thou hast made the heaven and the earth by thy great power and stretched out arm, and there is nothing too hard for thee: Jeremiah 32:17

He healeth the broken in heart, and bindeth up their wounds. He telleth the number of the stars; he calleth them all by their names. Great is our Lord, and of great power: his understanding is infinite. Psalm 147:3-5

God's power gives me hope.

May the God of hope fill you with all joy and peace in believing, so that by the power of the Holy Spirit you may abound in hope. Romans 15:13

OMNIPRESENT

God is everywhere present at all times.

The eyes of the Lord are in every place, beholding the evil and the good. Proverbs 15:3

Whither shall I go from thy spirit? or whither shall I flee from thy presence? If I ascend up into heaven, thou art there: if I make my bed in hell, behold, thou art there. If I take the wings of the morning, and dwell in the uttermost parts of the sea; Even there shall thy hand lead me, and thy right hand shall hold me. Psalm 139:7-10

Am I a God at hand, saith the Lord, and not a God afar off? Can any hide himself in secret places that I shall not see him? saith the Lord. Do not I fill heaven and earth? saith the Lord. Jeremiah 23:23-24

I am Alpha and Omega, the beginning and the ending, saith the Lord, which is, and which was, and which is to come, the Almighty. Revelation 1:8

OMNISCIENCE

God knows everything about me.

O Lord, thou hast searched me, and known me. Thou knowest my downsitting and mine uprising, thou understandest my thought afar off. Thou compassest my path and my lying down, and art acquainted with all my ways. For there is not a word in my tongue, but, lo, O Lord, thou knowest it altogether. Thou hast beset me behind and before, and laid thine hand upon me. Psalm 139:1-5

God knows when I am disobeying.

But if ye will not do so, behold, ye have sinned against the Lord: and be sure your sin will find you out. Numbers 32:23

God knows when I do right.

For the Lord knoweth the way of the righteous: but the way of the ungodly shall perish. Psalm 1:6

For the eyes of the Lord are over the righteous, and his ears are open unto their prayers: but the face of the Lord is against them that do evil. 1 Peter 3:12

O the depth of the riches both of the wisdom and knowledge of God! how unsearchable are his judgments, and his ways past finding out! For who hath known the mind of the Lord? or who hath been his counsellor? Or who hath first given to him, and it shall be recompensed unto him again? For of him, and through him, and to him, are all things: to whom be glory for ever. Amen. Romans 11:33-36

Parents

Godly parents are thrilled when their children learn to be wise.

The father of the righteous shall greatly rejoice: and he that begetteth a wise child shall have joy of him. Thy father and thy mother shall be glad, and she that bare thee shall rejoice. Proverbs 23:24-25

I have no greater joy than to hear that my children walk in truth. 3 John 1:4

And, ye fathers, provoke not your children to wrath: but bring them up in the nurture and admonition of the Lord. Ephesians 6:4

God wants parents to teach their children to love God's ways, grow up, and teach THEIR children to love God's ways!

We will not hide them from their children, shewing to the generation to come the praises of the Lord, and his strength, and his wonderful works that he hath done. For he established a testimony in Jacob, and appointed a law in Israel, which he commanded our fathers, that they should make them known to their children: Psalm 78:4-5

When my parents do not follow Christ, God will help me do right.

Can a woman forget her sucking child, that she should not have compassion on the son of her womb? yea, they may forget, yet will I not forget thee. Isaiah 49:15

When my father and my mother forsake me, then the Lord will take me up. Psalm 27:10

That the generation to come might know them [God's Teachings], The children who would be born, That they may arise and declare them to their children, That they may set their hope in God, And not forget the works of God, But keep His commandments; And may not be like their fathers, A stubborn and rebellious generation, A generation that did not set its heart aright, And whose spirit was not faithful to God. Psalm 78:6-8

God uses children who have bad parents and good parents. King Josiah had an ungodly father and grandfather, but he chose to follow God! (2 Kings 22:2, and 22:19)

Timothy had a godly mother and grandmother who taught him the Bible when he was young. (2 Timothy 1:5; 3:15)

PATIENCE

Related topics: Anger, Longsuffering

God is patient [longsuffering].

But thou, O Lord, art a God full of compassion, and gracious, long suffering, and plenteous in mercy and truth. Psalm 86:15

Because God is patient, I can be patient.

Rest in the Lord, and wait patiently for him. Psalm 37:7a

Now the God of patience and consolation grant you to be likeminded one toward another according to Christ Jesus. Romans 15:5

Follow after righteousness, godliness, faith, love, patience, meekness. 1 Timothy 6:11b

I, therefore, the prisoner of the Lord, beseech you that ye walk worthy of the vocation wherewith ye are called, With all lowliness and meekness, with longsuffering, forbearing one another in love; Ephesians 4:1-2

Be not hasty in thy spirit to be angry: for anger resteth in the bosom of fools. Ecclesiastes 7:9

I learn to be patient when I study and follow Christ's example of patience.

Looking unto Jesus the author and finisher of our faith; who for the joy that was set before him endured the cross, despising the shame, and is set down at the right hand of the throne of God. For consider him that endured such contradiction of sinners against himself, lest ye be wearied and faint in your minds. Hebrews 12:2-3

Because God is a righteous judge, I can give my case to God and believe that he will judge those who have wronged me and treated me badly.

For even hereunto were ye called: because Christ also suffered for us, leaving us an example, that ye should follow his steps: Who did no sin, neither was guile found in his mouth: Who, when he was reviled, reviled not again; when he suffered, he threatened not; but committed himself to him that judgeth righteously: 1 Peter 2:21-23

PEACE

All peace comes from God!

For unto us a child is born, unto us a son is given: and the government shall be upon his shoulder: His name shall be called Wonderful, Counsellor, The mighty God, The everlasting Father, The Prince of Peace. Isaiah 9:6

Grace and peace be multiplied unto you through the knowledge of God, and of Jesus our Lord. 2 Peter 1:2

But the fruit of the spirit is love, joy, peace... Galatians 5:22a

God first gives me peace when I become a Christian.
Therefore being justified by faith, we have peace with God through our Lord Jesus Christ. Romans 5:1

Now the God of hope fill you with all joy and peace in believing, that ye may abound in hope, through the power of the Holy Ghost. Romans 15:13

God gives peace to me as I learn to love the Bible.
Great peace have they which love thy law: and nothing shall offend them. Psalm 119:165

God gives peace to me as I think about how much God loves me and takes care of me!
Thou wilt keep him in perfect peace, whose mind is stayed on thee: because he trusteth in thee. Isaiah 26:3

Peace I leave with you, my peace I give unto you: not as the world giveth, give I unto you. Let not your heart be troubled, neither let it be afraid. John 14:27

God gives peace to me as I learn to pray.
Be careful for nothing; but in every thing by prayer and supplication with thanksgiving let your requests be made known unto God. And the peace of God, which passeth all understanding, shall keep your hearts and minds through Christ Jesus. Philippians 4:6-7

God gives peace to me as I learn to think about good things.
Finally, brethren, whatsoever things are true, whatsoever things are honest, whatsoever things are just, whatsoever things are pure, whatsoever things are lovely, whatsoever things are of good report; if there be any virtue, and if there be any praise, think on these things. Those things, which ye have both learned, and received, and heard, and seen in me, do: and the God of peace shall be with you. Philippians 4:8-9

PERSEVERANCE

See Give Up.

PETS

A righteous man regardeth the life of his beast: but the tender mercies of the wicked are cruel. Proverbs 12:10

For the scripture saith, thou shalt not muzzle the ox that treadeth out the corn. And, The labourer is worthy of his reward. 1 Timothy 5:18

> The Prophet Nathan told David a story about a pet lamb in order to teach him an important lesson. 2 Samuel 12:1-6

Prayer

God loves to hear Christians pray to him.

The sacrifice of the wicked is an abomination to the Lord: but the prayer of the upright is his delight. Proverbs 15:8

The eyes of the Lord are upon the righteous, and his ears are open unto their cry. Psalm 34:15

Ask, and it shall be given you; seek, and ye shall find; knock, and it shall be opened unto you: For every one that asketh receiveth; and he that seeketh findeth; and to him that knocketh it shall be opened. Or what man is there of you, whom if his son ask bread, will he give him a stone? Or if he ask a fish, will he give him a serpent? If ye then, being evil, know how to give good gifts unto your children, how much more shall your Father which is in heaven give good things to them that ask him? Matthew 7:7-11

God wants me to pray for help when I am in trouble.

And call upon me in the day of trouble: I will deliver thee, and thou shalt glorify me. Psalm 50:15

From the end of the earth will I cry unto thee, when my heart is overwhelmed: lead me to the rock that is higher than I. Psalm 61:2

Plead my cause, O Lord, with them that strive with me: fight against them that fight against me. Psalm 35:1

Let us therefore come boldly unto the throne of grace, that we may obtain mercy, and find grace to help in time of need. Hebrews 4:16

God tells me some things he wants me to pray for.

Pray ye therefore the Lord of the harvest, that he will send forth labourers into his harvest. Matthew 9:38

But I say unto you, Love your enemies, bless them that curse you, do good to them that hate you, and pray for them which despitefully use you, and persecute you; Matthew 5:44

Jesus gave an example of how to pray.

After this manner therefore pray ye: Our Father which art in heaven, Hallowed be thy name. Thy kingdom come, Thy will be done in earth, as it is in heaven. Give us this day our daily bread. And forgive us our debts, as we forgive our debtors. And lead us not into temptation, but deliver us from evil: For thine is the kingdom, and the power, and the glory, for ever. Amen. Matthew 6:9-13

Read some prayers that Paul prayed for his friends. Philippians 1:9-11; Colossians 1:9-11

John recorded a prayer Jesus prayed for me, in John 17:1-26. See verse 20

Rhoda was a little girl who prayed with her church that Peter would be released from jail. When God answered their prayers and Peter showed up, nobody in the church believed it was Peter except Rhoda! Acts 12:5-16

Pride

Related topic: Humility

I learn to stop being prideful as I learn to know God.

Talk no more so exceeding proudly; let not arrogancy come out of your mouth: for the Lord is a God of knowledge, and by him actions are weighed. 1 Samuel 2:3

The wicked, through the pride of his countenance, will not seek after God: God is not in all his thoughts. Psalm 10:4

Then said I, Woe is me! for I am undone; because I am a man of unclean lips, and I dwell in the midst of a people of unclean lips: for mine eyes have seen the King, the Lord of hosts. Isaiah 6:5

Because God hates pride, I am learning to hate it too!

These six things doth the Lord hate: yea, seven are an abomination unto him: A proud look, a lying tongue, and hands that shed innocent blood, An heart that deviseth wicked imaginations, feet that be swift in running to mischief, A false witness that speaketh lies, and he that soweth discord among brethren. Proverbs 6:16-19

Pride, and arrogancy, and the evil way, and the froward [stubbornly disobedient] mouth, do I hate. Proverbs 8:13b

For all that is in the world, the lust of the flesh, and the lust of the eyes, and the pride of life, is not of the Father, but is of the world. 1 John 2:16

Pride goeth before destruction, and an haughty spirit before a fall. Proverbs 16:18

God helps me fight pride by listening carefully.

Only by pride cometh contention: but with the well advised is wisdom. Proverbs 13:10

The way of a fool is right in his own eyes: but he that hearkeneth unto counsel is wise. Proverbs 12:15

God helps me fight pride by looking for wisdom and seeking God.

When pride cometh, then cometh shame: but with the lowly is wisdom. Proverbs 11:2

God helps me fight pride by stopping wrong thoughts and starting to think right thoughts.

For from within, out of the heart of men, proceed evil thoughts, adulteries, fornications, murders, thefts, covetousness, wickedness, deceit, lasciviousness, an evil eye, blasphemy, pride, foolishness: Mark 7:21-22

Casting down imaginations, and every high thing that exalteth itself against the knowledge of God, and bringing into captivity every thought to the obedience of Christ;
2 Corinthians 10:5

God helps me fight pride by loving others.

Knowledge puffeth up, but charity edifieth. 1 Corinthians 8:1

Wherefore let him that thinketh he standeth take heed lest he fall. 1 Corinthians 10:12

God helps me fight pride by serving others, and not comparing myself with others.

And he [Jesus] came to Capernaum: and being in the house he asked them, What was it that ye disputed among yourselves by the way? But they held their peace: for by the way they had disputed among themselves, who should be the greatest. And he sat down, and called the twelve, and saith unto them, If any man desire to be first, the same shall be last of all, and servant of all. Mark 9:33-35

God helps me fight pride by becoming thankful.
Because that, when they knew God, they glorified him not as God, neither were thankful; but became vain in their imaginations, and their foolish heart was darkened. Professing themselves to be wise, they became fools.
Romans 1:21-22

God helps me fight pride by submitting to authority.
But he giveth more grace. Wherefore he saith, God resisteth the proud, but giveth grace unto the humble. Submit yourselves therefore to God. Resist the devil, and he will flee from you. Draw nigh to God, and he will draw nigh to you. Cleanse your hands, ye sinners; and purify your hearts, ye double minded. James 4:6-8

King Nebuchadnezzar thought his success was all because he was so wonderful, but God caused him to lose his mind and act like an animal until he repented. Daniel 4:30-37

For more reading about humility, read Philippians 2:3-11.

Satan used to be an important angel who served God in Heaven. His pride caused him to rebel against God. Isaiah 14:12-15

PURITY

Even a child is known by his doings, whether his work be pure, and whether it be right. Proverbs 20:11

Because God has saved me, and is making me pure like Jesus, he wants me to care about keeping my heart clean from sin.

Beloved, now are we the sons of God, and it doth not yet appear what we shall be: but we know that, when he shall appear, we shall be like him; for we shall see him as he is. And every man that hath this hope in him purifieth himself, even as he is pure. 1 John 3:2-3

I learn to be pure when I obey the Bible

Wherewithal shall a young man cleanse his way? by taking heed thereto according to thy word. Psalm 119:9

I learn to be pure by keeping my thoughts right.

Keep thy heart with all diligence; for out of it are the issues of life. Proverbs 4:23

Finally, brethren, whatsoever things are true, whatsoever things are honest, whatsoever things are just, whatsoever things are pure, whatsoever things are lovely, whatsoever things are of good report; if there be any virtue, and if there be any praise, think on these things. Philippians 4:8

Casting down imaginations, and every high thing that exalteth itself against the knowledge of God, and bringing into captivity every thought to the obedience of Christ; 2 Corinthians 10:5

I learn to be pure by avoiding sin.

I will set no wicked thing before mine eyes: I hate the work of them that turn aside; it shall not cleave to me. Psalm 101:3

But Daniel purposed in his heart that he would not defile himself with the portion of the king's meat, nor with the wine which he drank: therefore he requested of the prince of the eunuchs that he might not defile himself. Daniel 1:8

And I find more bitter than death the woman, whose heart is snares and nets, and her hands as bands: whoso pleaseth God shall escape from her; but the sinner shall be taken by her. Ecclesiastes 7:26

I learn to be pure by becoming wise!

For the commandment is a lamp; and the law is light; and reproofs of instruction are the way of life: to keep thee from the evil woman, from the flattery of the tongue of a strange woman. Proverbs 6:23-24

RAIN

Are there any among the vanities of the cause rain? or can the heavens give showers? art not thou he, O Lord our God? therefore we will wait upon thee: for thou hast made all these things. Jeremiah 14:22

Also by watering he wearieth the thick cloud: he scattereth his bright cloud: And it is turned round about by his counsels: that they may do whatsoever he commandeth them upon the face of the world in the earth. He causeth it to come, whether for correction, or for his land, or for mercy. Job 37:11-13

He [Jesus] answered and said unto them, When it is evening, ye say, It will be fair weather: for the sky is red. And in the morning, It will be foul weather to day: for the sky is red and lowering. O ye hypocrites, ye can discern the face of the sky; but can ye not discern the signs of the times? Matthew 16:2-3

Rejection

Related topic: Lonely

Sometimes friends act like enemies and reject us.

For it was not an enemy that reproached me; then I could have borne it: neither was it he that hated me that did magnify himself against me; then I would have hid myself from him: But it was thou, a man mine equal, my guide, and mine acquaintance. We took sweet counsel together, and walked unto the house of God in company. Psalm 55:12-14

Sometimes we feel lonely when friends reject us.

My lovers and my friends stand aloof from my sore; and my kinsmen stand afar off. Psalm 38:11

At my first answer no man stood with me, but all men forsook me: I pray God that it may not be laid to their charge. 2 Timothy 4:16.

Jesus tells me not to worry about being rejected, because he will never reject me.

Blessed are ye, when men shall hate you, and when they shall separate you from their company, and shall reproach you, and cast out your name as evil, for the Son of man's sake. Luke 6:22

And whosoever will not receive you, when ye go out of that city, shake off the very dust from your feet for a testimony against them. Luke 9:5

What shall we then say to these things? If God be for us, who can be against us? Romans 8:31

When my father and my mother forsake me, then the Lord will take me up. Psalm 27:10

And the Lord shall deliver me from every evil work, and will preserve me unto his heavenly kingdom: to whom be glory for ever and ever. Amen. 2 Timothy 4:18

REMEMBER

Related topic: Forget

Remembering helps me do right!

Some trust in chariots, and some in horses; But we will remember the name of the Lord our God. Psalm 20:7

Therefore if thou bring thy gift to the altar, and there rememberest that thy brother hath ought against thee; Leave there thy gift before the altar, and go thy way; first be reconciled to thy brother, and then come and offer thy gift. Matthew 5:23-24

Remember now thy Creator in the days of thy youth, while the evil days come not, nor the years draw nigh, when thou shalt say, I have no pleasure in them; Ecclesiastes 12:1

Meditating about what I remember helps me not to forget.

When I remember thee upon my bed, and meditate on thee in the night watches. Psalm 63:6

I remember the days of old; I meditate on all thy works; I muse on the work of thy hands. I stretch forth my hands unto thee: my soul thirsteth after thee, as a thirsty land. Selah. Psalm 143:5-6

This book of the law shall not depart out of thy mouth; but thou shalt meditate therein day and night, that thou mayest observe to do according to all that is written therein: for then thou shalt make thy way prosperous, and then thou shalt have good success. Joshua 1:8

Talking about what I remember helps me not to forget.

Rejoice in the Lord, ye righteous: and give thanks at the remembrance of his holiness. Psalm 97:12

I will make thy name to be remembered in all generations: therefore shall the people praise thee for ever and ever. Psalm 45:17

Repentance

Related topic: Sin

The angels in heaven rejoice when I repent!

Likewise, I say unto you, there is joy in the presence of the angels of God over one sinner that repenteth. Luke 15:10

When I see how loving and patient God is, I want to repent!

Or despisest thou the riches of his goodness and forbearance and longsuffering; not knowing that the goodness of God leadeth thee to repentance? Romans 2:4

Let the wicked forsake his way, and the unrighteous man his thoughts: and let him return unto the Lord, and he will have mercy upon him; and to our God, for he will abundantly pardon. Isaiah 55:7

God promises that he will always forgive me when I repent!

If we confess our sins, he is faithful and just to forgive us our sins, and to cleanse us from all unrighteousness. 1 John 1:9

He that covereth his sins shall not prosper: but whoso confesseth and forsaketh them shall have mercy. Proverbs 28:13

For more reading about repentance, read Psalms 32 and 51. King David wrote these poems when he repented of his sin.

Read some examples of people who repented: the whole church at Corinth, 2 Corinthians 7:9-11; the prodigal son, Luke 15:11-32; Jonah, Jonah 1-4.

Respect

God wants me to respect my parents.

Children, obey your parents in the Lord: for this is right. Honour thy father and mother; which is the first commandment with promise; That it may be well with thee, and thou mayest live long on the earth. Ephesians 6:1-3

God wants me to respect others.

Be kindly affectioned one to another with brotherly love; in honour preferring one another; Romans 12:10

Honour all men. Love the brotherhood. Fear God. Honour the king. 1 Peter 2:17

Let nothing be done through strife or vainglory; but in lowliness of mind let each esteem other better than themselves. Look not every man on his own things, but every man also on the things of others. Philippians 2:3-4

> The Rechabites were praised for respecting their grandfather's instructions even after they were grown. Jeremiah 35:13-19
>
> Rehoboam did not respect the wise counsel of the older men, but instead followed the foolish counsel of his friends. 1 Kings 12

Sadness

Related topics: Disappointment, Prayer, Hope, Give Up, Worry

All the solutions to my sadness will not last unless my hope is in God. (See Omniscience.)

Some trust in chariots, and some in horses: but we will remember the name of the Lord our God. Psalm 20:7

From the end of the earth will I cry unto thee, when my heart is overwhelmed: lead me to the rock that is higher than I. For thou hast been a shelter for me, and a strong tower from the enemy. Psalm 61:2-3

I cried unto the Lord with my voice; with my voice unto the Lord did I make my supplication. I poured out my complaint before him; I shewed before him my trouble. When my spirit was overwhelmed within me, then thou knewest my path. Psalm 142:1-3a

When I am sad, I am helped by remembering that God loves me. (See God, Hope.)

Casting all your care upon him; for he careth for you. 1 Peter 5:7

Are not five sparrows sold for two farthings, and not one of them is forgotten before God? But even the very hairs of your head are all numbered. Fear not therefore: ye are of more value than many sparrows. Luke 12:6-7

Blessed are they that mourn: for they shall be comforted. Matthew 5:4

When I am sad, I am helped by remembering that God controls all things. (See Omnipotence, Disappointment.)

For promotion cometh neither from the east, nor from the west, nor from the south. But God is the judge: he putteth down one, and setteth up another. Psalm 75:6-7

And we know that all things work together for good to them that love God, to them who are the called according to his purpose. Romans 8:28

When I don't know why I am sad or cannot think of the words to pray, the Holy Spirit prays the right words for me! (See Prayer.)

Likewise the Spirit also helpeth our infirmities: for we know not what we should pray for as we ought: but the Spirit itself maketh intercession for us with groanings which cannot be uttered. And he that searcheth the hearts knoweth what is the mind of the Spirit, because he maketh intercession for the saints according to the will of God. Romans 8:26-27

Why art thou cast down, O my soul? and why art thou disquieted in me? hope thou in God: for I shall yet praise him for the help of his countenance. Deep calleth unto deep at the noise of thy waterspouts: all thy waves and thy billows are gone over me. Yet the Lord will command his lovingkindness in the day time, and in the night his song shall be with me, and my prayer unto the God of my life. Psalm 42:5, 7-8

Sometimes I am sad because I have been lazy or not doing right. I am helped when I do right. (See Work, Chores, Repentance, Sin.)

Slothfulness casteth into a deep sleep; and an idle soul shall suffer hunger. Proverbs 19:15

It is good and comely for one to eat and to drink, and to enjoy the good of all his labour that he taketh under the sun all the days of his life, which God giveth him: for it is his portion. Ecclesiastes 5:18

Blessed is he whose transgression is forgiven! Psalm 32:1a

When I feel like giving up, I am helped by remembering Jesus' example, and his faithfulness to finish his work in my life. (See Give Up, Hope.)

Being confident of this very thing, that he which hath begun a good work in you will perform it until the day of Jesus Christ: Philippians 1:6

Wherefore seeing we also are compassed about with so great a cloud of witnesses, let us lay aside every weight, and the sin which doth so easily beset us, and let us run with patience the race that is set before us, Looking unto Jesus the author and finisher of our faith; who for the joy that was set before him endured the cross, despising the shame, and is set down at the right hand of the throne of God. Hebrews 12:1-2

Jesus still felt sadness even though he was doing right. Mark 14:34-36

Elijah was sad because he felt like he was the only one doing right. He also wasn't eating or sleeping well. 1 Kings 19:3-6

Job didn't understand why God was allowing problems in his life. He was helped by learning more about God. Job 23:8-10, and chapters 38-41. See Job's answer to God in Job 42:5-6.

Jonah was sad and angry because he did not want to do right. God wanted him to repent. Jonah 4

SALVATION

Related topics: Sin, Repentance

For God so loved the world, that he gave his only begotten Son, that whosoever believeth in him should not perish, but have everlasting life. John 3:16

And they said, Believe on the Lord Jesus Christ, and thou shalt be saved, and thy house. Acts 16:31

That if thou shalt confess with thy mouth the Lord Jesus, and shalt believe in thine heart that God hath raised him from the dead, thou shalt be saved. For with the heart man believeth unto righteousness; and with the mouth confession is made unto salvation. Romans 10:9-10

When God's children are saved, they tell others that God has saved them.

Whosoever therefore shall confess me before men, him will I confess also before my Father which is in heaven. Matthew 10:32

The angels in heaven see and are happy whenever a little child is saved!

Likewise, I say unto you, there is joy in the presence of the angels of God over one sinner that repenteth. Luke 15:10

I am saved and kept saved by the power of God!

All that the Father giveth me shall come to me; and him that cometh to me I will in no wise cast out. John 6:37

But as many as received him, to them gave he power to become the sons of God, even to them that believe on his name: John 1:12

For I know whom I have believed, and am persuaded that he is able to keep that which I have committed unto him against that day. 2 Timothy 1:12

Being confident of this very thing, that he which hath begun a good work in you will perform it until the day of Jesus Christ: Philippians 1:6

A saved child knows that he is becoming more like Christ.

Beloved, now are we the sons of God, and it doth not yet appear what we shall be: but we know that, when he shall appear, we shall be like him; for we shall see him as he is. And every man that hath this hope in him purifieth himself, even as he is pure. 1 John 3:2-3

God's Word teaches me that I will stay in his hands and love, no matter what.

My sheep hear my voice, and I know them, and they follow me: And I give unto them eternal life; and they shall never perish, neither shall any man pluck them out of my hand. John 10:27-28

Nay, in all these things we are more than conquerors through him that loved us. For I am persuaded, that neither death, nor life, nor angels, nor principalities, nor powers, nor things present, nor things to come, Nor height, nor depth, nor any other creature, shall be able to separate us from the love of God, which is in Christ Jesus our Lord. Romans 8:37-39

Having a clean conscience (finding forgiveness) helps me to be sure I am saved!

Let us draw near [to God] with a true heart in full assurance of faith, having our hearts sprinkled from an evil conscience, and our bodies washed with pure water. Let us hold fast the profession of our faith without wavering; (for he is faithful that promised;) Hebrews 10:22-23

And beside this, giving all diligence, add to your faith virtue; and to virtue knowledge; And to knowledge temperance; and to temperance patience; and to patience godliness; And to godliness brotherly kindness; and to brotherly kindness charity. For if these things be in you, and abound, they make you that ye shall neither be barren nor unfruitful in the knowledge of our Lord Jesus Christ. But he that lacketh these things is blind, and cannot see afar off, and hath forgotten that he was purged from his old sins. 2 Peter 1:5-9

SCHOOL

I can learn to be faithful by studying hard in school, even when school is difficult or boring.

And he said unto him, Well, thou good servant: because thou hast been faithful in a very little, have thou authority over ten cities. Luke 19:17

Seest thou a man diligent in his business? He shall stand before kings; he shall not stand before mean men. Proverbs 22:29

Study to shew thyself approved unto God, a workman that needeth not to be ashamed, rightly dividing the word of truth. 2 Timothy 2:15

Whoso loveth instruction loveth knowledge: but he that hateth reproof is brutish. Proverbs 12:1

Whatsoever thy hand findeth to do, do it with thy might; for there is no work, nor device, nor knowledge, nor wisdom, in the grave, whither thou goest. Ecclesiastes 9:10

I am sometimes tired of studying, but the most important thing to learn is to fear God and obey him.

Only take heed to thyself, and keep thy soul diligently, lest thou forget the things which thine eyes have seen, and lest they depart from thy heart all the days of thy life: but teach them thy sons, and thy sons' sons; Deuteronomy 4:9

And further, by these, my son, be admonished: of making many books there is no end; and much study is a weariness of the flesh. Let us hear the conclusion of the whole matter: Fear God, and keep his commandments: for this is the whole duty of man. Ecclesiastes 12:12-13

People in the Bible who used their education: Solomon (1 Kings 4:32-34); Paul (Acts 17:28 and 22:3); Ezra (Ezra 7:10); Moses (Acts 7:22)

SELF-CONTROL

Related topics: Contentment, Listening, Patience, Selfish

Self control comes from the Holy Spirit when I obey God's Word.

But the fruit of the Spirit is love, joy, peace, longsuffering, gentleness, goodness, faith, Meekness, temperance [self control]: against such there is no law. Galatians 5:22-23

Self-control helps me avoid a lot of trouble!

He that hath no rule over his own spirit is like a city that is broken down, and without walls. Proverbs 25:28

Whoso keepeth his mouth and his tongue keepeth his soul from troubles. Proverbs 21:23

Hast thou found honey? eat so much as is sufficient for thee, lest thou be filled therewith, and vomit it. Proverbs 25:16

He that is slow to anger is better than the mighty; and he that ruleth his spirit than he that taketh a city. Proverbs 16:32

Let all things be done decently and in order.
1 Corinthians 14:40

Learning self control takes God's work in my life as well as hard work!

And beside this, giving all diligence, add to your faith virtue; and to virtue knowledge; And to knowledge temperance; and to temperance patience. 2 Peter 1:5-6a

What? know ye not that your body is the temple of the Holy Ghost which is in you, which ye have of God, and ye are not your own? For ye are bought with a price: therefore glorify God in your body, and in your spirit, which are God's. 1 Corinthians 6:19-20

That ye put off concerning the former conversation the old man, which is corrupt according to the deceitful lusts; And be renewed in the spirit of your mind; And that ye put on the new man, which after God is created in righteousness and true holiness. Ephesians 4:22-24

When I choose to be patient with God's timing, I am learning self-control.

Wait on the Lord: be of good courage, and he shall strengthen thine heart: wait, I say, on the Lord. Psalm 27:14

But, beloved, be not ignorant of this one thing, that one day is with the Lord as a thousand years, and a thousand years as one day. 2 Peter 3:8

The Lord is not slack concerning his promise, as some men count slackness; but is longsuffering to us-ward, not willing that any should perish, but that all should come to repentance. 2 Peter 3:9

SELF ESTEEM

Related topics: Shy, Confidence

God wants me to see myself truthfully.

For I say, through the grace given unto me, to every man that is among you, not to think of himself more highly than he ought to think; but to think soberly, according as God hath dealt to every man the measure of faith. Romans 12:3

I will praise thee; for I am fearfully and wonderfully made: marvellous are thy works; and that my soul knoweth right well. My substance was not hid from thee, when I was made in secret, and curiously wrought in the lowest parts of the earth. Thine eyes did see my substance, yet being unperfect; and in thy book all my members were written, which in continuance were fashioned, when as yet there was none of them. Psalm 139:14-16

God will help me do ANYTHING he wants me to do.

I can do all things through Christ which strengtheneth me. Philippians 4:13

God wants me to pray and ask him for help when I need it.

Let us therefore come boldly unto the throne of grace, that we may obtain mercy, and find grace to help in time of need. Hebrews 4:16

God is powerful, and my weaknesses are no trouble for him.

And he said unto me, My grace is sufficient for thee: for my strength is made perfect in weakness. Most gladly therefore will I rather glory in my infirmities, that the power of Christ may rest upon me. Therefore I take pleasure in infirmities, in reproaches, in necessities, in persecutions, in distresses for Christ's sake: for when I am weak, then am I strong. 2 Corinthians 12:9-10

For I know the thoughts that I think toward you, saith the Lord, thoughts of peace, and not of evil, to give you an expected end. Jeremiah 29:11

He delighteth not in the strength of the horse: he taketh not pleasure in the legs of a man. The Lord taketh pleasure in them that fear him, in those that hope in his mercy.
Psalm 147:10-11

Jesus shows me that he wants me to think about others more than myself.

Let nothing be done through strife or vainglory; but in lowliness of mind let each esteem other better than themselves. Look not every man on his own things, but every man also on the things of others. Let this mind be in you, which was also in Christ Jesus: Who, being in the form of God, thought it not robbery to be equal with God. But made himself of no reputation, and took upon him the form of a servant, and was made in the likeness of men: And being found in fashion as a man, he humbled himself, and became obedient unto death, even the death of the cross. Philippians 2:3-8

SELFISH

Related topics: Pride, Humility

Jesus wants me to fight me-first attitudes by learning to serve others.

And he [Jesus] came to Capernaum: and being in the house he asked them, What was it that ye disputed among yourselves by the way? But they held their peace: for by the way they had disputed among themselves, who should be the greatest. And he sat down, and called the twelve, and saith unto them, If any man desire to be first, the same shall be last of all, and servant of all. Mark 9:33-35

Let nothing be done through strife or vainglory; but in lowliness of mind let each esteem other better than themselves. Look not every man on his own things, but every man also on the things of others. Philippians 2:3-4

Even as the Son of man came not to be ministered unto, but to minister, and to give his life a ransom for many. Matthew 20:28

God wants me to stop having a me-first attitude and help those who are weak.

We then that are strong ought to bear the infirmities of the weak, and not to please ourselves. Let every one of us please his neighbour for his good to edification. For even Christ pleased not himself. Romans 15:1-3a

> For examples of people in the Bible who were selfish, read here: Ahab and Naboth (1 Kings 21:1-19); Haman (Esther 6:6); Satan (Isaiah 14:12-14); Ananias and Sapphira (Acts 5:1-11).

SHY

Related topics: Self Esteem, Confidence, Fear of God

Because God made me, I do not have to be afraid of people.

Then the word of the Lord came unto me, saying, Before I formed thee in the belly I knew thee; and before thou camest forth out of the womb I sanctified thee, and I ordained thee a prophet unto the nations. Then said I, Ah, Lord God! behold, I cannot speak: for I am a child. But the Lord said unto me, Say not, I am a child: for thou shalt go to all that I shall send thee, and whatsoever I command thee thou shalt speak. Be not afraid of their faces: for I am with thee to deliver thee, saith the Lord. Jeremiah 1:4-8

And Moses said unto the Lord, O my Lord, I am not eloquent, neither heretofore, nor since thou hast spoken unto thy servant: but I am slow of speech, and of a slow tongue. And the Lord said unto him, Who hath made man's mouth? or who maketh the dumb, or deaf, or the seeing, or the blind? have not I the Lord? Now therefore go, and I will be with thy mouth, and teach thee what thou shalt say. Exodus 4:10-12

Fear of what people think of us is a trap that we can avoid when we learn to trust and fear God.

The fear of man bringeth a snare: but whoso putteth his trust in the Lord shall be safe. Proverbs 29:25

What time I am afraid, I will trust in thee. In God I will praise his word, in God I have put my trust; I will not fear what flesh can do unto me. Psalm 56:3-4

In whom [Jesus] we have boldness and access with confidence by the faith of him. Ephesians 3:12

God wants even shy children to do good works that others can see!

Let your light so shine before men, that they may see your good works, and glorify your Father which is in heaven. Matthew 5:16

SIN

Related topics: Repentance, Salvation

Sin is not living up to God's glory.

For all have sinned, and come short of the glory of God; Romans 3:23

Whosoever committeth sin transgresseth also the law: for sin is the transgression of the law. And ye know that he was manifested to take away our sins; and in him is no sin. 1 John 3:4-5

Because God sees everything, I cannot hide my sin from God.

Be sure your sin will find you out. Numbers 32:23b

When Christians sin, God helps them to make things right with him again.

If we say that we have no sin, we deceive ourselves, and the truth is not in us. If we confess our sins, he is faithful and just to forgive us our sins, and to cleanse us from all unrighteousness. 1 John 1:8-9

For a just man falleth seven times, and riseth up again: Proverbs 24:16a

The steps of a good man are ordered by the Lord: and he delighteth in his way. Though he fall, he shall not be utterly cast down: for the Lord upholdeth him with his hand. Psalm 37:23-24

God has given me tools to help me keep from sin.

Thy word have I hid in mine heart, that I might not sin against thee. Psalm 119:11

Confess your faults one to another, and pray one for another, that ye may be healed. The effectual fervent prayer of a righteous man availeth much. James 5:16

That ye put off concerning the former conversation the old man, which is corrupt according to the deceitful lusts; And be renewed in the spirit of your mind; And that ye put on the new man, which after God is created in righteousness and true holiness. Ephesians 4:22-24

God always gives me a way to escape sin!

There hath no temptation taken you but such as is common to man: but God is faithful, who will not suffer you to be tempted above that ye are able; but will with the temptation also make a way to escape, that ye may be able to bear it. 1 Corinthians 10:13

God loves me and is quick to forgive me when i sin!

For thou, Lord, art good, and ready to forgive;
and plenteous in mercy unto all them that call upon thee. Psalm 86:5

The Lord is merciful and gracious, slow to anger, and plenteous in mercy. Psalm 103:8

As far as the east is from the west, so far hath he removed our transgressions from us. Like as a father pitieth his children, so the Lord pitieth them that fear him. Psalm 103:12-13

God always forgives me when I ask him to.

If we confess our sins, he is faithful and just to forgive us our sins, and to cleanse us from all unrighteousness. 1 John 1:9

Who is a God like unto thee, that pardoneth iniquity, and passeth by the transgression of the remnant of his heritage? he retaineth not his anger for ever, because he delighteth in mercy. He will turn again, he will have compassion upon us; he will subdue our iniquities; and thou wilt cast all their sins into the depths of the sea. Micah 7:18-19

Sleep

I am helped when I go to sleep by thinking about the wonderful works of God!

I will both lay me down in peace, and sleep: for thou, Lord, only makest me dwell in safety. Psalm 4:8

Yet the Lord will command his lovingkindness in the daytime, and in the night his song shall be with me, and my prayer unto the God of my life. Psalm 42:8

My soul shall be satisfied as with marrow and fatness; and my mouth shall praise thee with joyful lips: When I remember thee upon my bed, and meditate on thee in the night watches. Because thou hast been my help, therefore in the shadow of thy wings will I rejoice. Psalm 63:5-7

It is vain for you to rise up early, to sit up late, to eat the bread of sorrows: for so he giveth his beloved sleep. Psalm 127:2

Sleep can be a bad thing if it is too much or at the wrong time.

He that gathereth in summer is a wise son: but he that sleepeth in harvest is a son that causeth shame. Proverbs 10:5

How long wilt thou sleep, O sluggard? when wilt thou arise out of thy sleep? Yet a little sleep, a little slumber, a little folding of the hands to sleep: Proverbs 6:9-10

God never sleeps; he is always ready to help!

I will lift up mine eyes unto the hills, from whence cometh my help. My help cometh from the Lord, which made heaven and earth. He will not suffer thy foot to be moved: he that keepeth thee will not slumber. Behold, he that keepeth Israel shall neither slumber nor sleep. Psalm 121:1-4

Rest is a result of trust and obedience.

Rest in the Lord, and wait patiently for him: fret not thyself because of him who prospereth in his way, because of the man who bringeth wicked devices to pass. Psalm 37:7

Thus saith the Lord, Stand ye in the ways, and see, and ask for the old paths, where is the good way, and walk therein, and ye shall find rest for your souls. But they said, We will not walk therein. Jeremiah 6:16

Come unto me, all ye that labour and are heavy laden, and I will give you rest. Take my yoke upon you, and learn of me; for I am meek and lowly in heart: and ye shall find rest unto your souls. For my yoke is easy, and my burden is light. Matthew 11:28-30

Even in Bible times people sometimes grew tired with long preaching. Eutychus fell asleep and fell out a window! Acts 20:9-12

SPORTS

And if a man also strive for masteries, yet is he not crowned, except he strive lawfully. 2 Timothy 2:5

For by thee I have run through a troop; and by my God have I leaped over a wall. As for God, his way is perfect: the word of the Lord is tried: he is a buckler to all those that trust in him. Psalm 18:29-30

The Bible teaches that being a Christian is like being in a race.

Know ye not that they which run in a race run all, but one receiveth the prize? So run, that ye may obtain. And every man that striveth for the mastery is temperate in all things. Now they do it to obtain a corruptible crown; but we an incorruptible. I therefore so run, not as uncertainly; so fight I, not as one that beateth the air: But I keep under my body, and bring it into subjection: lest that by any means, when I have preached to others, I myself should be a castaway. 1 Corinthians 9:24-27

A good athlete (and a good Christian) learns when to forget about past failures and victories. Instead he thinks about the game he is playing now.

Brethren, I count not myself to have apprehended: but this one thing I do, forgetting those things which are behind, and reaching forth unto those things which are before, I press toward the mark for the prize of the high calling of God in Christ Jesus. Philippians 3:13-14

God rewards Christians who work patiently and don't give up!

I have fought a good fight, I have finished my course, I have kept the faith: Henceforth there is laid up for me a crown of righteousness, which the Lord, the righteous judge, shall give me at that day: and not to me only, but unto all them also that love his appearing. 2 Timothy 4:7-8

Wherefore seeing we also are compassed about with so great a cloud of witnesses, let us lay aside every weight, and the sin which doth so easily beset us, and let us run with patience the race that is set before us, Looking unto Jesus the author and finisher of our faith; who for the joy that was set before him endured the cross, despising the shame, and is set down at the right hand of the throne of God. For consider him that endured such contradiction of sinners against himself, lest ye be wearied and faint in your minds.
Hebrews 12:1-3

STARS

The stars show God's greatness and goodness.

The heavens declare the glory of God; and the firmament sheweth his handywork. Day unto day uttereth speech, and night unto night sheweth knowledge. There is no speech nor language, where their voice is not heard. Psalm 19:1-3

God is so big that he knows all the stars, and he also knows and cares when I am hurting.

He healeth the broken in heart, and bindeth up their wounds. He telleth the number of the stars; he calleth them all by their names. Great is our Lord, and of great power: his understanding is infinite. Psalm 147:3-5

I follow the creator of the stars.

[God], Which alone spreadeth out the heavens, and treadeth upon the waves of the sea. Which maketh Arcturus, Orion, and Pleiades, and the chambers of the south. Which doeth great things past finding out; yea, and wonders without number. Job 9:8-10

Seek him that maketh the seven stars and Orion, and turneth the shadow of death into the morning, and maketh the day dark with night: that calleth for the waters of the sea, and poureth them out upon the face of the earth: The Lord is his name: Amos 5:8

STEALING

Related topics: Giving, Work, Contentment

Ye shall not steal, neither deal falsely, neither lie one to another. Leviticus 19:11

A child who wants to stop stealing must learn to work and give to others.

Let him that stole steal no more: but rather let him labour, working with his hands the thing which is good, that he may have to give to him that needeth. Ephesians 4:28

A child who wants to stop stealing must learn to change how he thinks, and be content!

Incline my heart unto thy testimonies, and not to covetousness. Psalm 119:36

Let your conversation be without covetousness; and be content with such things as ye have: for he hath said, I will never leave thee, nor forsake thee. Hebrews 13:5

And he said, That which cometh out of the man, that defileth the man. For from within, out of the heart of men, proceed evil thoughts, adulteries, fornications, murders, Thefts, covetousness, wickedness, deceit, lasciviousness, an evil eye, blasphemy, pride, foolishness: Mark 7:20-22

Suffering

Because God cares for me, he will help me when I go through difficult things

Fear thou not; for I am with thee: be not dismayed; for I am thy God: I will strengthen thee; yea, I will help thee; yea, I will uphold thee with the right hand of my righteousness. Isaiah 41:10

Casting all your care upon him; for he careth for you. 1 Peter 5:7

For I know the thoughts that I think toward you, saith the Lord, thoughts of peace, and not of evil, to give you an expected end. Jeremiah 29:11

There will be no suffering in heaven.

And [in heaven] God shall wipe away all tears from their eyes; and there shall be no more death, neither sorrow, nor crying, neither shall there be any more pain: for the former things are passed away. Revelation 21:4

We are troubled on every side, yet not distressed; we are perplexed, but not in despair; Persecuted, but not forsaken; cast down, but not destroyed; Always bearing about in the body the dying of the Lord Jesus, that the life also of Jesus might be made manifest in our body. 2 Corinthians 4:8-10

God expects believers to treat children with kindness and respect.

And whoso shall receive one such little child in my name receiveth me. But whoso shall offend one of these little ones which believe in me, it were better for him that a millstone were hanged about his neck, and that he were drowned in the depth of the sea. Matthew 18:5-6

Because God comforts me, I can be like him when I comfort others who are suffering too.

[God] comforteth us in all our tribulation, [so] that we may be able to comfort them which are in any trouble, by the comfort wherewith we ourselves are comforted of God.
2 Corinthians 1:4

For which cause we faint not; but though our outward man perish, yet the inward man is renewed day by day. For our light affliction, which is but for a moment, worketh for us a far more exceeding and eternal weight of glory; While we look not at the things which are seen, but at the things which are not seen: for the things which are seen are temporal; but the things which are not seen are eternal.
2 Corinthians 4:16-18

God loves me, even when I make wrong choices.

Who shall separate us from the love of Christ? shall tribulation, or distress, or persecution, or famine, or nakedness, or peril, or sword? As it is written, For thy sake we are killed all the day long; we are accounted as sheep for the slaughter. Nay, in all these things we are more than conquerors through him that loved us. For I am persuaded, that neither death, nor life, nor angels, nor principalities, nor powers, nor things present, nor things to come, Nor height, nor depth, nor any other creature, shall be able to separate us from the love of God, which is in Christ Jesus our Lord. Romans 8:35-39

Paul used the laws of Rome to protect himself.

And the keeper of the prison told this saying to Paul, The magistrates have sent to let you go: now therefore depart, and go in peace. But Paul said unto them, They have beaten us openly uncondemned, being Romans, and have cast us into prison; and now do they thrust us out privily? nay verily; but let them come themselves and fetch us out. And the serjeants told these words unto the magistrates: and they feared, when they heard that they were Romans.
Acts 16:36-38

God gave government and laws to punish evildoers and protect his children.

Submit yourselves to every ordinance of man for the Lord's sake: whether it be to the king, as supreme; Or unto governors, as unto them that are sent by him for the punishment of evildoers, and for the praise of them that do well.
1 Peter 2:13-14

> See also how Paul reported wrongdoing to the authorities to protect himself: Acts 23:16-35.

TALKING

Sometimes it is good to learn to be quiet!

Whoso keepeth his mouth and his tongue keepeth his soul from troubles. Proverbs 21:23

And that ye study to be quiet, and to do your own business, and to work with your own hands, as we commanded you;
1 Thessalonians 4:11

Wherefore, my beloved brethren, let every man be swift to hear, slow to speak, slow to wrath: James 1:19

In the multitude of words there wanteth not sin: but he that refraineth his lips is wise. Proverbs 10:19

God's children learn not to criticize others.

He that is void of wisdom despiseth his neighbor: but a man of understanding holdeth his peace. Proverbs 11:12

God's children learn to use words to encourage others.

Heaviness in the heart of man maketh it stoop: but a good word maketh it glad. Proverbs 12:25

Let no corrupt communication proceed out of your mouth, but that which is good to the use of edifying, that it may minister grace unto the hearers. Ephesians 4:29

The right word at the right time is beautiful.

A word fitly spoken is like apples of gold in pictures of silver. Proverbs 25:11

A man hath joy by the answer of his mouth: and a word spoken in due season, how good is it! Proverbs 15:23

The preacher sought to find out acceptable words: and that which was written was upright, even words of truth. The words of the wise are as goads, and as nails fastened by the masters of assemblies, which are given from one shepherd. Ecclesiastes 12:10-11

Teasing

Bad teasing makes others look foolish because they do not see or understand the joke.

Thou shalt not curse the deaf, nor put a stumblingblock before the blind, but shalt fear thy God: I am the Lord. Leviticus 19:14

Bad teasing laughs at sin.

Neither filthiness, nor foolish talking, nor jesting, which are not convenient: but rather giving of thanks. Ephesians 5:4

Bad teasing is hurtful. Saying "I'm just joking" doesn't make it okay.

As a mad man who casteth firebrands, arrows, and death, So is the man that deceiveth his neighbour, and saith, Am not I in sport? Proverbs 26:18-19

Good teasing is kind, and enjoyed by both people.

Therefore all things whatsoever ye would that men should do to you, do ye even so to them: Matthew 7:12

Look not every man on his own things, but every man also on the things of others. Philippians 2:4

A merry heart doeth good like a medicine: but a broken spirit drieth the bones. Proverbs 17:22

Good teasing is at the right time.

[There is] a time to weep, and a time to laugh; a time to mourn, and a time to dance; Ecclesiastes 3:4

A B C D E F G H I J K L M N O P Q R S T U V W X Y Z

Thankfulness

In everything give thanks: for this is the will of God in Christ Jesus concerning you. 1 Thessalonians 5:18

One way I can say thank you to God is by telling my friends about God's goodness!

I will sing of the mercies of the Lord forever: with my mouth will I make known thy faithfulness to all generations. Psalm 89:1

Rejoice in the Lord, ye righteous: and give thanks at the remembrance of his holiness. Psalm 97:12

Godly people are thankful people.

Let the word of Christ dwell in you richly in all wisdom; teaching and admonishing one another in psalms and hymns and spiritual songs, singing with grace in your hearts to the Lord. And whatsoever ye do in word or deed, do all in the name of the Lord Jesus, giving thanks to God and the Father by him. Colossians 3:16-17

Because God loves me so much, I say thank you to God when I pray!

Continue in prayer and watch in the same with thanksgiving. Colossians 4:2

Be careful for nothing; but in everything by prayer and supplication with thanksgiving let your requests be made known unto God. Philippians 4:6

By him therefore let us offer the sacrifice of praise to God continually, that is, the fruit of our lips giving thanks to his name. Hebrews 13:15

It is a good thing to give thanks unto the Lord, and to sing praises unto thy name, O most High: To shew forth thy lovingkindness in the morning, and thy faithfulness every night. For thou, Lord, has made me glad through thy work: I will triumph in the works of thy hands. Psalm 92:1-2, 4

I will mention the lovingkindnesses of the Lord, and the praises of the Lord, according to all that the Lord hath bestowed on us, and the great goodness toward the house of Israel, which he hath bestowed on them according to his mercies, and according to the multitude of his lovingkindnesses. Isaiah 63:7

King David shows me a good example to start my prayer and worship with thanksgiving and praise.

Enter into his gates with thanksgiving, and into his courts with praise: be thankful unto him, and bless his name. Psalm 100:4

Blessed be the Lord, who daily loadeth us with benefits, even the God of our salvation. Psalm 68:19

I will be glad and rejoice in thy mercy: for thou hast considered my trouble; thou hast known my soul in adversities; Blessed be the Lord: for he hath shewed me his marvelous kindness in a strong city. Psalm 31:7

Oh how great is thy goodness, which thou hast laid up for them that fear thee; which thou hast wrought for them that trust in thee before the sons of men! Psalm 31:19

Trial/ Trouble

See Suffering

TRUST

Related topics: Faith, Omnipotence

Trust in the Lord with all thine heart; and lean not unto thine own understanding. In all thy ways acknowledge him, and he shall direct thy paths. Proverbs 3:5-6

For thou art my hope, O Lord God: thou art my trust from my youth. Psalm 71:5

The power and goodness of God makes it so that I can trust him.

The Lord is my strength and my shield; my heart trusted in him, and I am helped: therefore my heart greatly rejoiceth; and with my song will I praise him. Psalm 28:7

As for God, his way is perfect: the word of the Lord is tried: he is a buckler [shield] to all those that trust in him. Psalm 18:30

When I trust God, and he helps me, my heart sings for joy.

But let all those that put their trust in thee rejoice: let them ever shout for joy, because thou defendest them: let them also that love thy name be joyful in thee. Psalm 5:11

O taste and see that the Lord is good: blessed is the man that trusteth in him. Psalm 34:8

Trusting things, people, and even myself, is foolish!

He that trusteth in his riches shall fall; but the righteous shall flourish as a branch. Proverbs 11:28

He that trusteth in his own heart is a fool: but whoso walketh wisely, he shall be delivered. Proverbs 28:26

Thus saith the Lord; Cursed be the man that trusteth in man, and maketh flesh his arm, and whose heart departeth from the Lord. Jeremiah 17:5

Truth Telling

Related topic: Lying

Because Jesus is truth, I must tell the truth to be right with God.

Jesus saith unto him, I am the way, the truth, and the life: no man cometh unto the Father, but by me. John 14:6

God delights in us when we tell the truth!

They that deal truly are his delight. Proverbs 12:22b

King David prayed that God would help him to tell the truth.

Remove from me the way of lying: and grant me thy law graciously. I have chosen the way of truth: thy judgments have I laid before me. Psalm 119:29-30

He that covereth his sins shall not prosper: but whoso confesseth and forsaketh them shall have mercy. Proverbs 28:13

The person who is living truthfully loves to be near the light of God and his word. The person who lives a lie stays away from the light of God and his word.

For every one that doeth evil hateth the light, neither cometh to the light, lest his deeds should be reproved. But he that doeth truth cometh to the light, that his deeds may be made manifest, that they are wrought in God. John 3:20-21

When someone else is lying, I should remember that God sees all the secrets, and he reveals them in his time.

Daniel answered and said, Blessed be the name of God for ever and ever: for wisdom and might are his: And he changeth the times and the seasons: he removeth kings, and setteth up kings: he giveth wisdom unto the wise, and knowledge to them that know understanding: He revealeth the deep and secret things: he knoweth what is in the darkness, and the light dwelleth with him. Daniel 2:20-22

Because I will publish the name of the Lord: ascribe ye greatness unto our God. He is the Rock, his work is perfect: for all his ways are judgment: a God of truth and without iniquity, just and right is he. Deuteronomy 32:3-4

Moreover as for me, God forbid that I should sin against the Lord in ceasing to pray for you: but I will teach you the good and the right way: Only fear the Lord, and serve him in truth with all your heart: for consider how great things he hath done for you. 1 Samuel 12:23-24

WAR

Related topic: Suffering

Fights and wars are bad. They come from selfish and prideful desires.

Only by pride cometh contention: but with the well advised is wisdom. Proverbs 13:10

From whence come wars and fightings among you? come they not hence, even of your lusts that war in your members? Ye lust, and have not: ye kill, and desire to have, and cannot obtain: ye fight and war, yet ye have not, because ye ask not. James 4:1-2

God's people sometimes learn to use weapons, but they ask God to protect them.

For I will not trust in my bow, neither shall my sword save me. But thou hast saved us from our enemies, and hast put them to shame that hated us. Psalm 44:6-7

Blessed be the Lord my strength which teacheth my hands to war, and my fingers to fight: My goodness, and my fortress; my high tower, and my deliverer; my shield, and he in whom I trust; who subdueth my people under me. Psalm 144:1-2

Woe to them that go down to Egypt for help; and stay on horses, and trust in chariots, because they are many; and in horsemen, because they are very strong; but they look not unto the Holy One of Israel, neither seek the Lord! Isaiah 31:1

God shows his power by creating Leviathan, who was not threatened by the weapons of men.

The sword of him that layeth at him [the monster Leviathan] cannot hold: the spear, the dart, nor the habergeon. He esteemeth iron as straw, and brass as rotten wood. The arrow cannot make him flee: slingstones are turned with him into stubble. Darts are counted as stubble: he laugheth at the shaking of a spear. Job 41:26-29

God is my commander in chief, and my job is to please him in spiritual battle.

Thou therefore endure hardness, as a good soldier of Jesus Christ. No man that warreth entangleth himself with the affairs of this life; that he may please him who hath chosen him to be a soldier. 2 Timothy 2:3-4

Wherefore take unto you the whole armour of God, that ye may be able to withstand in the evil day, and having done all, to stand. Stand therefore, having your loins girt about with truth, and having on the breastplate of righteousness; And your feet shod with the preparation of the gospel of peace; Above all, taking the shield of faith, wherewith ye shall be able to quench all the fiery darts of the wicked. And take the helmet of salvation, and the sword of the Spirit, which is the word of God: Ephesians 6:13-17

King David was a warrior who loved and served God. 1 Samuel 17:49-51

Read about other skilled warriors that served God. 1 Chronicles 12:1-3, 12:8-15

The Centurion was a soldier of great faith. Luke 7:2-9

Will of God

Related topic: Wisdom

Because God has changed my heart, I want to do his will!

Many, O Lord my God, are thy wonderful works which thou hast done, and thy thoughts which are to us-ward: they cannot be reckoned up in order unto thee: if I would declare and speak of them, they are more than can be numbered. I delight to do thy will, O my God: yea, thy law is within my heart. Psalm 40:5, 8

Wisdom helps me to know God's will.

Wherefore be ye not unwise, but understanding what the will of the Lord is. Ephesians 5:17

Because God is kind and loves me, I trust he will answer me when I pray and ask him about his will.

Cause me to hear thy lovingkindness in the morning; for in thee do I trust: cause me to know the way wherein I should walk; for I lift up my soul unto thee. Psalm 143:8

Teach me to do thy will; for thou art my God: thy spirit is good; lead me into the land of uprightness. Psalm 143:10

Trust in the Lord with all your heart, And lean not on your own understanding; In all your ways acknowledge Him, And He shall direct your paths. Proverbs 3:5-6

God's will is for me to obey with the right attitude!

Servants, be obedient to them that are your masters according to the flesh, with fear and trembling, in singleness of your heart, as unto Christ; Not with eyeservice, as menpleasers; but as the servants of Christ, doing the will of God from the heart; Ephesians 6:5-6

In everything give thanks, for this is the will of God in Christ Jesus concerning you! 1 Thessalonians 5:18

Because God is merciful, he changes me. Then I can find God's will by filling my mind with good things.

I beseech you therefore, brethren, by the mercies of God, that ye present your bodies a living sacrifice, holy, acceptable unto God, which is your reasonable service. And be not conformed to this world: but be ye transformed by the renewing of your mind, that ye may prove what is that good, and acceptable, and perfect, will of God. Romans 12:1-2

Wisdom

Related topic: Will of God

God loves to give wisdom, and he wants me to ask him for it!

If any of you lack wisdom, let him ask of God, that giveth to all men liberally, and upbraideth not; and it shall be given him. James 1:5

Wisdom is better than anything I could ever want!

For wisdom is better than rubies; and all the things that may be desired are not to be compared to it. Proverbs 8:11

My son, eat thou honey, because it is good; and the honeycomb, which is sweet to thy taste: so shall the knowledge of wisdom be unto thy soul: when thou hast found it, then there shall be a reward, and thy expectation shall not be cut off. Proverbs 24:13-14

Jesus teaches that the way to be wise is to hear God's Word, and also obey it.

Therefore whosoever heareth these sayings of mine, and doeth them, I will liken him unto a wise man, which built his house upon a rock. Matthew 7:24

The fear of the Lord is the beginning of wisdom: a good understanding have all they that do his commandments: his praise endureth for ever. Psalm 111:10

Learning God's words without obeying them is not wise. It is foolish!

And every one that heareth these sayings of mine, and doeth them not, shall be likened unto a foolish man, which built his house upon the sand. Matthew 7:26

King Solomon wrote the book of Proverbs so children like me could learn to be wise.

The proverbs of Solomon the son of David, king of Israel; To know wisdom and instruction; to perceive the words of understanding; Proverbs 1:1-2

Fake wisdom might sound good, but it looks bad.

But if ye have bitter envying and strife in your hearts, glory not, and lie not against the truth. This wisdom descendeth not from above, but is earthly, sensual, devilish. For where envying and strife is, there is confusion and every evil work. James 3:14-16

True wisdom isn't just good words. It results in good actions, too.

But the wisdom that is from above is first pure, then peaceable, gentle, and easy to be intreated, full of mercy and good fruits, without partiality, and without hypocrisy. And the fruit of righteousness is sown in peace of them that make peace. James 3:17-18

When God told Solomon to make a wish for whatever he wanted, Solomon asked for wisdom (1 Kings 3:5-10). God was so pleased that he made Solomon the wisest man who ever lived (1 Kings 4:29-34).

WORK

Related Topics: Chores, School, Give Up

And whatsoever ye do, do it heartily, as to the Lord, and not unto men; Colossians 3:23

God created my body and mind to be able to work. Work is a blessing, and not a curse!

There is nothing better for a man, than that he should eat and drink, and that he should make his soul enjoy good in his labour. This also I saw, that it was from the hand of God. Ecclesiastes 2:24

And the Lord God took the man [Adam], and put him into the garden of Eden to dress it and to keep it. Genesis 2:15

God uses the ant to teach me how to work hard without being told.

Go to the ant, thou sluggard; consider her ways, and be wise: Which having no guide, overseer, or ruler, provideth her meat in the summer, and gathereth her food in the harvest. Proverbs 6:6-8

God wants me to learn diligent and honest work.

And that ye study to be quiet, and to do your own business, and to work with your own hands, as we commanded you; That ye may walk honestly toward them that are without, and that ye may have lack of nothing. 1 Thessalonians 4:11-12

Seest thou a man diligent in his business? he shall stand before kings; he shall not stand before mean men. Proverbs 22:29

Lazy people make excuses instead of working.

The sluggard will not plow by reason of the cold; therefore shall he beg in harvest, and have nothing. Proverbs 20:4

The slothful man saith, There is a lion without, I shall be slain in the streets. Proverbs 22:13

God has chosen work to provide for my needs.

For even when we were with you, this we commanded you, that if any would not work, neither should he eat. For we hear that there are some which walk among you disorderly, working not at all, but are busybodies. Now them that are such we command and exhort by our Lord Jesus Christ, that with quietness they work, and eat their own bread. But ye, brethren, be not weary in well doing. 2 Thessalonians 3:10-13

The slothful man roasteth not that which he took hunting: but the substance of a diligent man is precious. Proverbs 12:27

God rested after he worked, and wants me to rest after I work!

And on the seventh day God ended his work which he had made; and he rested on the seventh day from all his work which he had made. And God blessed the seventh day, and sanctified it: because that in it he had rested from all his work which God created and made. Genesis 2:2-3

God sees and rewards the hard work of his children.

Therefore, my beloved brethren, be ye stedfast, unmoveable, always abounding in the work of the Lord, forasmuch as ye know that your labour is not in vain in the Lord. 1 Corinthians 15:58

For God is not unrighteous to forget your work and labour of love, which ye have shewed toward his name, in that ye have ministered to the saints, and do minister. And we desire that every one of you do shew the same diligence to the full assurance of hope unto the end: That ye be not slothful, but followers of them who through faith and patience inherit the promises. Hebrews 6:10-12

WORRY

Related topic: Afraid

Therefore take no thought, saying, What shall we eat? or, What shall we drink? or, Wherewithal shall we be clothed? (For after all these things do the Gentiles seek:) for your heavenly Father knoweth that ye have need of all these things. Matthew 6:31-32

But seek ye first the kingdom of God, and his righteousness; and all these things shall be added unto you. Take therefore no thought for the morrow: for the morrow shall take thought for the things of itself. Sufficient unto the day is the evil thereof. Matthew 6:33-34

It is vain for you to rise up early, to sit up late, to eat the bread of sorrows: for so he giveth his beloved sleep. Psalm 127:2

When I worry, God teaches me to pray.

Be careful for nothing; but in every thing by prayer and supplication with thanksgiving let your requests be made known unto God. And the peace of God, which passeth all understanding, shall keep your hearts and minds through Christ Jesus. Philippians 4:6-7

God's Children learn to think about good things instead of worry!

Finally, brethren, whatsoever things are true, whatsoever things are honest, whatsoever things are just, whatsoever things are pure, whatsoever things are lovely, whatsoever things are of good report; if there be any virtue, and if there be any praise, think on these things. Those things, which ye have both learned, and received, and heard, and seen in me, do: and the God of peace shall be with you. Philippians 4:8-9

Zeal

Good zeal is energy and eagerness to do right.

Ye know the house of Stephanas, that it is the firstfruits of Achaia, and that they have addicted themselves to the ministry of the saints. 1 Corinthians 16:15

Looking for that blessed hope, and the glorious appearing of the great God and our Saviour Jesus Christ; Who gave himself for us, that he might redeem us from all iniquity, and purify unto himself a peculiar people, zealous of good works. Titus 2:13-14

King Josiah had zeal to do right, even when he was only eight years old! God blessed his tender and humble heart. II Chronicles 34

God used Nehemiah to share his zeal to rebuild the temple! Nehemiah 2:17-20

10 Ways to Use the Book

- *Topical Bible for Kids* can be used as a tool for family devotions. Children or parents can pick a topic for discussion, and then read, discuss, or memorize the verses for that topic together. Any of the following recommendations can also be implemented as hands-on family devotion activities.
- My friend Emily secretly chooses a topic, does a sword drill of the references with her children, and has them guess the topic. Then they discuss the verses. (This is a great way to use the book with different Bible translations.)
- During mealtime discussions or car trips, ask children to identify topics and verses that they like. I like to ask, "What is God teaching you? What are your favorite verses on that topic?" Sometimes I bring up a topic to start the conversation: "What verses comfort you when you are sad?" "Would you like to find some verses together that will be a help to you?" These questions and follow-up study help them see that the Bible is an enjoyable resource for life and delight, and not a club of punishment.
- Using this book as a starting point, help children write out favorite verses in a handmade book, or on index cards to tape on their wall next to their beds. They may enjoy making and printing "business cards" with topics, verses, and clip art. These also make good gifts.
- Help young children find and highlight verses they have memorized. These are the easiest verses for new and struggling readers to find in the Bible and read. Read the topics from the table of contents and ask them to stop you when they are interested in finding verses on that topic. Then, encourage them to highlight their favorite verses in their Bibles.
- Consider allowing children to stay up late, if they are reading or listening to their Bible in their rooms. Teach them that a child doesn't have to be a good reader to love and obey the Bible!

- If children are looking for topics not included in this book, show them how to search for new topics online (such as at biblegateway.com), or with a concordance. Help them collect verses on their interests.
- Help children make a chain of verses in their Bibles by writing the next reference on a topic in the margin. Making connections is one way children (and parents) learn to be active and happy students of God's Word.
- Help children identify Bible synonyms and key words for topics by circling the words in the text that correspond to the topic. (For example, in the topic "Fighting," Bible words include strife, wars, contention.)
- Help children identify Bible opposites as they study: fighting and forgiveness, complain and contentment, and so on. Many opposites are already given as cross references in the text.

This book is a gift to my three children: David, Bethel, and Laurel, with the prayer that they continue to learn to love God and His Word with all their hearts.

Thank you to my husband, Lee, who has encouraged me and supported me throughout this project. He is the one who pushed me to invest in new software, who helped me over the initial shock of learning a new program, language and procedures, and who solved the really big problems when I got stuck. He brought home red licorice and gummi bears many times and kept up the supply of fresh roasted coffee in spite of his own busy schedule. Thank you for making this book possible!

Thank you to my brother Thomas Pryde, and Jay Younts, for their encouragement, and the hours they gave providing theological feedback for this project.

Thank you also to Laura Weimer, Deborah Hawkins, Denise Franklin, Emily Helmick, and others who read early versions and gave valuable feedback from a mother's perspective.

I am also grateful to my parents, who have shown me all my life what it looks like to delight in God and his word.

We will not hide them from their children, shewing to the generation to come the praises of the Lord, and his strength, and his wonderful works that he hath done.

For he established a testimony in Jacob, and appointed a law in Israel, which he commanded our fathers, that they should make them known to their children:

That the generation to come might know them, even the children which should be born; who should arise and declare them to their children: Psalm 78:4-6

A
B
C
D
E
F
G
H
I
J
K
L
M
N
O
P
Q
R
S
T
U
V
W
X
Y
Z

A
B
C
D
E
F
G
H
I
J
K
L
M
N
O
P
Q
R
S
T
U
V
W
X
Y
Z

A
B
C
D
E
F
G
H
I
J
K
L
M
N
O
P
Q
R
S
T
U
V
W
X
Y
Z

Made in the USA
Lexington, KY
14 November 2019

57045667R00100